SCHOLASTIC

GRADE 4

Morning Jumpstarts:
READING

100 Independent Practice Pages to Build Essential Skills

Marcia Miller & Martin Lee

New York • Toronto • ney

Mexico City • New Delhi • Hong Kong • Buenos Aires

Edited by Mela Ottaiano
Cover design by Michelle H. Kim
Interior design by Sydney Wright
"Swift Things Are Beautiful" is used by permission of the Marsh Agency Ltd.
on behalf of the Estate of Elizabeth Coatsworth.
Interior illustrations by Teresa Anderko, Maxie Chambliss, Mike Gordon,
James Graham Hale, and Sydney Wright; © 2013 by Scholastic Inc.
Image credits: Cover photo © Jacob Wackerhausen/Thinkstock; page 14 © Stapleton Collection/Corbis;
page 20 © Pacific Stock-Design Pic/SuperStock; pages 30 and 50 © iStockphoto; page 44 © Alison Wright/Corbis;
page 56 © Stockagogo/Big Stock Photo; page 60 © Bettmann/Corbis; page 68 © Paul A. Souders/Corbis;
page 92 © Photosindia.com/SuperStock. All images © 2013.
ISBN: 978-0-545-46423-9
Copyright © 2013 by Scholastic Inc.
Published by Scholastic Inc. All rights reserved.
Printed in the U.S.A.
First printing, January 2013.
4 5 6 7 8 9 10   40   21 20 19 18 17 16

Contents

Introduction 4

How to Use This Book 5

A Look Inside 6

Connections to the Common Core State Standards 7

Jumpstarts 1–50 9

Answers 109

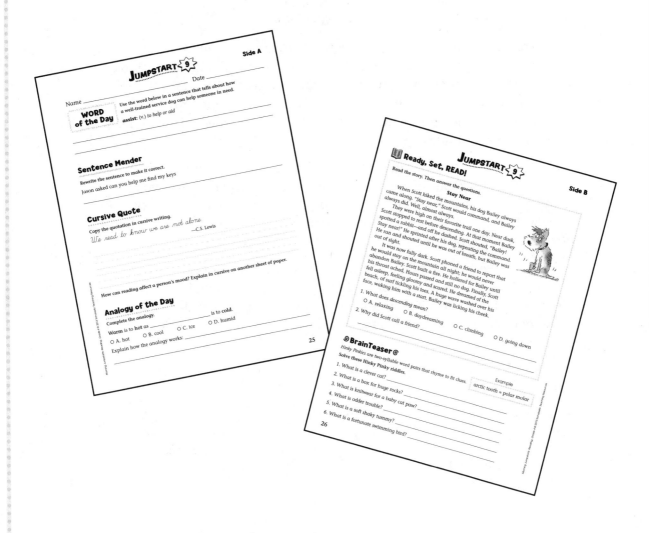

Introduction

In your busy classroom, you know how vital it is to energize students for the tasks of the day. That's why *Morning Jumpstarts: Reading, Grade 4* is the perfect tool for you.

The activities in this book provide brief and focused individual practice in grade-level skills students are expected to master. Each Jumpstart is a two-page collection of six activities designed to review and reinforce a range of reading and writing skills students will build throughout the year. The consistent format helps students work independently and with confidence. Each Jumpstart includes these features:

- Word of the Day
- Sentence Mender
- Cursive Quote
- Analogy of the Day
- Ready, Set, Read!
- Brainteaser

You can use a Jumpstart in its entirety or, because each feature is self-contained, assign sections at different times of the day or to different groups of learners. The Jumpstart activities will familiarize students with the kinds of challenges they will encounter on standardized tests, and provide a review of skills they need to master. (See page 6 for a close-up look at the features in each Jumpstart.)

The Common Core State Standards (CCSS) for English Language Arts serve as the backbone of the activities in this book. On pages 7–8, you'll find a correlation chart that details how the 50 Jumpstarts dovetail with the widely accepted set of guidelines for preparing students to succeed in reading and language arts.

Generally, we have kept in mind the CCSS "anchor standards" that should inform solid instruction in reading literary and informational texts. In addition, the activity pages provide students with practice in developing and mastering foundational and language skills, summarized below.

ANCHOR STANDARDS FOR READING	FOUNDATIONAL SKILLS	LANGUAGE
• Key Ideas and Details • Craft and Structure • Integration of Knowledge and Ideas • Range of Reading and Level of Text Complexity	• Phonics and Word Recognition • Fluency	• Conventions of Standard English • Knowledge of Language • Vocabulary Acquisition and Use

Morning Jumpstarts: Reading, Grade 4 © 2013 Scholastic Teaching Resources

How to Use This Book

Morning Jumpstarts: Reading, Grade 4 can be used in many ways—and not just in the morning! You know your students best, so feel free to pick and choose among the activities, and incorporate those you see fit. You can make double-sided copies, or print one side at a time and staple the pages together.

We suggest the following times to present Jumpstarts:

- At the start of the school day, as a way to help students settle into the day's routines.
- Before lunch, as students ready themselves for their midday break.
- After lunch, as a calming transition into the afternoon's plans.
- Toward the end of the day, before students gather their belongings to go home, or for homework.

In general, the Jumpstarts progress in difficulty level and build on skills covered in previous sheets. Preview each one before you assign it, to ensure that students have the skills needed to complete them. Keep in mind, however, that you may opt for some students to skip sections, as appropriate, or complete them together at a later time as part of a small-group or whole-class lesson.

Undoubtedly, students will complete their Jumpstart activity pages at different rates. We suggest that you set up a "what to do when I'm done" plan to give students who need more time a chance to finish without interruption. For example, you might encourage students to complete another Jumpstart. They might also choose to read silently, practice handwriting, journal, or engage in other kinds of writing.

An answer key begins on page 109. You might want to review answers with the whole class. This approach provides opportunities for discussion, comparison, extension, reinforcement, and correlation to other skills and lessons in your current plans. Your observations can direct the kinds of review or reinforcement you may want to add to your lessons. Alternatively, you may find that having students discuss activity solutions and strategies in small groups is another effective approach.

When you introduce the first Jumpstart, walk through its features with your class to provide an overview before you assign it and to make sure students understand the directions. Help students see that the activities in each section focus on different kinds of skills, and let them know that the same sections will repeat throughout each Jumpstart, always in the same order and position. You might want to work through the first few Jumpstarts as a group until students are comfortable with the routine and ready to work independently.

You know best how to assign the work to the students in your class. You might, for instance, stretch a Jumpstart over two days, assigning Side A on the first day and Side B on the second. Although the activities on different Jumpstarts vary in difficulty and in time needed, we anticipate that once students are familiar with the routine, most will be able to complete both sides of a Jumpstart in anywhere from 10 to 20 minutes.

A Look Inside

Each two-page Jumpstart includes the following skill-building features.

Word of the Day The first feature on Side A builds vocabulary. Students read a grade-appropriate word and its definition. A brief writing task asks them to use the new word to demonstrate understanding of its proper usage.

Sentence Mender The second Side A feature addresses grade-appropriate conventions of standard English, especially spelling, capitalization, grammar, and punctuation. Students will see a sentence with errors. Their task is to rewrite the sentence correctly. A sample answer is given in the answer key, but it is quite possible that students may devise alternate corrections. Link this task to the revising and proofreading steps of the writing process.

Cursive Quote This feature offers students a chance to practice cursive handwriting as they copy and think about a quotation. Students will then write a response to a question that is based on the quote. For this task, direct students to use another sheet of paper, their writing journals, or the back of the Jumpstart sheet if only copied on one side. This section may serve as a springboard for discussion, further study, or correlation with other curriculum areas.

Analogy of the Day Every Side A concludes with an analogy that has one missing term. The key is for students to determine the relationship that links the first two words, and then choose the word that will create a second pair of words that relate in the same way. They will also write a description of the relationship. The Jumpstarts present a range of at least a dozen different types of analogies, such as part-whole relationships, object-action, object-description, example-class, antonyms, and so on.

Ready, Set, Read! Every Side B begins with a brief reading passage, followed by two or more text-based questions. Passages include fiction and nonfiction, prose and poetry, serious and humorous writing, realistic and fantastical settings. Dig deeper into any passage to inspire discussion, questions, and extension.

Tell students to first read the passage and then answer the questions. If necessary, show them how to fill in the circles for multiple-choice questions. For questions that require student to write, encourage them to use another sheet of paper, if needed.

Brainteaser Side B always ends with some form of an entertaining word or language challenge: a puzzle, code, riddle, or other engaging, high-interest task designed to stretch the mind. While some students may find this section particularly challenging, others will relish teasing out tricky solutions. This feature also provides another chance for group work or discussion. It may prove useful to have pairs of students tackle these together. And, when appropriate, invite students to create their own challenges, using ideas sparked by these exercises. Feel free to create your own variations of any brainteasers your class enjoys.

Morning Jumpstarts: Reading, Grade 4 © 2013 Scholastic Teaching Resources

Connections to the Common Core State Standards

As shown in the chart below and on page 8, the activities in this book will help you meet your specific state reading and language arts standards as well as those outlined in the CCSS. These materials address the following standards for students in grade 4. For details on these standards, visit the CCSS Web site: www.corestandards.org/the-standards/.

JS	4.RL.1	4.RL.2	4.RL.3	4.RL.4	4.RL.5	4.RL.6	4.RL.7	4.RL.9	4.RL.10	4.RI.1	4.RI.2	4.RI.3	4.RI.4	4.RI.5	4.RI.6	4.RI.7	4.RI.8	4.RI.10	4.RF.3	4.RF.4	4.L.1	4.L.2	4.L.3	4.L.4	4.L.5	4.L.6
1	•	•	•	•					•										•	•	•	•	•	•	•	•
2										•	•	•	•				•	•		•	•	•	•	•	•	•
3	•	•	•	•	•			•	•										•	•	•	•	•	•	•	•
4										•	•	•	•	•		•	•	•	•	•	•	•	•	•	•	•
5	•	•	•	•				•	•										•	•	•	•	•	•	•	•
6										•	•		•	•		•		•	•	•	•	•	•	•	•	•
7	•	•			•	•	•		•										•	•	•	•	•	•	•	•
8										•	•	•	•						•	•	•	•	•	•	•	•
9	•	•	•	•	•				•										•	•	•	•	•	•	•	•
10										•	•		•	•	•	•	•	•	•	•	•	•	•	•	•	•
11	•	•		•				•	•										•	•	•	•	•	•	•	•
12										•	•		•	•					•	•	•	•	•	•	•	•
13	•	•	•	•		•		•	•										•	•	•	•	•	•	•	•
14										•	•	•	•	•			•	•	•	•	•	•	•	•	•	•
15	•	•	•	•			•		•										•	•	•	•	•	•	•	•
16										•	•	•	•	•		•	•	•	•	•	•	•	•	•	•	•
17	•	•	•		•			•	•										•	•	•	•	•	•	•	•
18										•	•	•	•			•	•	•	•	•	•	•	•	•	•	•
19	•	•		•				•	•										•	•	•	•	•	•	•	•
20										•	•	•	•				•	•	•	•	•	•	•	•	•	•
21	•	•	•	•	•	•	•	•	•										•	•	•	•	•	•	•	•
22										•	•		•		•		•	•	•	•	•	•	•	•	•	•
23										•	•	•	•			•	•		•	•	•	•	•	•	•	•
24										•		•	•			•	•		•	•	•	•	•	•	•	•
25	•	•	•	•					•										•	•	•	•	•		•	•

Reading: Literature columns: 4.RL.1–4.RL.10. *Reading: Informational Text* columns: 4.RI.1–4.RI.10. *Reading: Foundational Skills* columns: 4.RF.3, 4.RF.4. *Language* columns: 4.L.1–4.L.6.

JS	4.RL.1	4.RL.2	4.RL.3	4.RL.4	4.RL.5	4.RL.6	4.RL.7	4.RL.9	4.RL.10	4.RI.1	4.RI.2	4.RI.3	4.RI.4	4.RI.5	4.RI.6	4.RI.7	4.RI.8	4.RI.10	4.RF.3	4.RF.4	4.L.1	4.L.2	4.L.3	4.L.4	4.L.5	4.L.6
						Reading: Literature								Reading: Informational Text						Reading: Foundational Skills				Language			
26										•	•	•	•	•			•	•	•	•	•	•	•	•	•	•
27	•	•	•	•	•			•	•										•	•	•	•	•	•	•	•
28										•	•		•			•		•	•	•	•	•	•	•	•	•
29	•	•	•	•	•	•			•										•	•	•	•	•	•	•	•
30										•	•	•	•	•		•	•	•	•	•	•	•	•	•	•	•
31	•	•	•	•	•				•										•	•	•	•	•	•	•	•
32										•	•	•	•	•	•	•	•	•	•	•	•	•	•	•	•	•
33	•	•	•	•	•	•	•		•										•	•	•	•	•	•	•	•
34										•	•		•				•	•	•	•	•	•	•	•	•	•
35	•	•	•		•			•	•										•	•	•	•	•	•	•	•
36										•	•	•	•	•	•	•		•	•	•	•	•	•	•	•	•
37										•	•	•	•			•	•	•	•			•	•	•	•	•
38										•	•	•	•	•	•	•		•	•	•	•	•	•	•	•	•
39	•	•	•	•		•		•	•										•	•	•	•	•	•	•	•
40										•	•	•		•	•		•	•	•	•	•	•	•	•	•	•
41										•	•	•		•		•	•	•	•	•	•	•	•	•	•	•
42										•	•	•		•		•	•	•	•	•	•	•	•	•	•	•
43	•	•		•					•										•	•	•	•	•	•	•	•
44										•	•	•	•		•	•	•	•	•	•	•	•	•	•	•	•
45	•	•	•			•	•		•										•	•	•	•	•	•	•	•
46										•	•	•	•				•	•		•	•	•	•	•	•	•
47										•	•	•				•	•		•	•	•	•	•	•	•	•
48										•	•	•	•			•	•	•	•	•	•	•	•	•	•	•
49	•	•	•	•					•										•	•		•	•	•	•	•
50										•	•						•	•			•		•		•	•

Morning Jumpstarts: Reading, Grade 4 © 2013 Scholastic Teaching Resources

Name _____ Date _____

WORD of the Day

Use the word below in a sentence about a daily habit that helps you get ready for school.

routine: (n.) *a regular or usual way to do things; habit*

_____

_____

Sentence Mender

Rewrite the sentence to make it correct.

Are 3 puppys our Mo Curly and Larry

_____

Cursive Quote

Copy the quotation in cursive writing.

Every path has its puddle.

—Anonymous

_____

_____

_____

Do you agree with this proverb? Write your answer in cursive on another sheet of paper.

Analogy of the Day

Complete the analogy.

Flower is to **garden** as _____ is to **playground**.

O A. desk   O B. school   O C. park   O D. slide

Explain how the analogy works: _____

_____

 # Ready, Set, READ!

Read the story. Then answer the questions.

Picking a Pup

Mom and I were so excited as we arrived at the animal shelter. We couldn't wait to pick our new puppy. An employee soon approached us carrying a tiny ball of fluff under each arm. She smiled and led us into a tiny room. She left us there with both pups and said, "They're sisters. Take all the time you need." She closed the door and left us with two adorable mutts. How would we ever decide? They looked like twins.

One scampered right over and jumped on us. She chewed on my sneaker laces and licked my face. Mom and I were smiling our heads off. While this frisky pup was nibbling on my fingers, her sister was moving slowly around the edges of the room. She sniffed at each corner. Next she came to sniff us, too. Then she sat by our feet, looked up at us, and rolled onto her back for a tummy rub.

We made our choice.

1. What were the "tiny balls of fluff" the employee carried?

_____

_____

2. What choice do you think they made? Explain.

_____

_____

ꙩ BrainTeaser ꙩ

Climb the word ladder to change *lamp* to *fire*. Change only one letter at a time. Write the new word on each step.

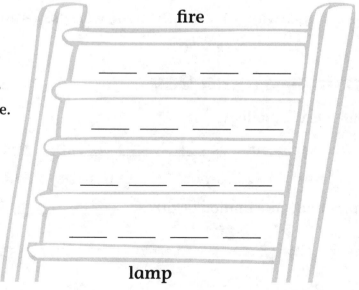

fire

lamp

Morning Jumpstarts: Reading, Grade 4 © 2013 Scholastic Teaching Resources

Name _____ Date _____

WORD of the Day

Use the word below in a sentence about the basic goal of a sport or game you enjoy.

basic: (adj.) *main part; at the root of; underlying; primary*

_____

_____

Sentence Mender

Rewrite the sentence to make it correct.

can you name all fivety States of the united states

_____

Cursive Quote

Copy the quotation in cursive writing.

A half truth is a whole lie.

—Jewish proverb

....

- -

....

What does this saying mean? Write your answer in cursive on another sheet of paper.

Analogy of the Day

Complete the analogy.

Flat is to **level** as _____ is to **large**.

○ A. small   ○ B. big   ○ C. straight   ○ D. tiny

Explain how the analogy works: _____

_____

📖 Ready, Set, READ!

Read the e-mail. Then answer the questions.

> Hey Trey,
>
> My dad is taking Katy and me apple picking on Saturday. He says you can come, too, if it's okay with your mom. The apple orchard is less than an hour away, past a waterfall and a llama ranch. Dad loves fresh apples (and I love apple pie!), so he needs some willing farmhands!
>
> Apple picking isn't hard work. In fact, it's pretty fun. I've done it before, so I know. Plus it's active, tasty, AND can be quite messy! Oh, did I mention the bonus? On the way back, we usually stop at this great ice-cream stand. They have maybe ten flavors, but each one is so creamy, your mouth will faint!
>
> Please let me know by tomorrow, if you can. If you can't come, I'll invite another friend. But you're my first choice, pal.
>
> Randy

1. What do farmhands do?

_____

_____

2. What does Randy mean by telling Trey that his *mouth will faint*?

_____

_____

ᓚ BrainTeaser ᓈ

Use the clues to complete a word that starts with *sho*.

1. Footwear   S H O ___ ___

2. Rattled   S H O ___ ___

3. Coastline   S H O ___ ___

4. Ought to   S H O ___ ___ ___

5. Place to wash off S H O ___ ___ ___

6. Tools for digging S H O ___ ___ ___

Morning Jumpstarts: Reading, Grade 4 © 2013 Scholastic Teaching Resources

Name _____ Date _____

WORD of the Day

Use the word below in a sentence to describe something you recite or sing in this way.

chant: (v.) *to sing or say over and over again in rhythm*

_____

_____

Sentence Mender

Rewrite the sentence to make it correct.

No I did not eet the last peace of candie

_____

Cursive Quote

Copy the quotation in cursive writing.

Never, never, never give up.

—Sir Winston Churchill

_____

_____

_____

_____

Explain why Churchill's advice could be hard to follow. Write your explanation in cursive on another sheet of paper.

Analogy of the Day

Complete the analogy.

Hungry is to **eat** as _____ is to **cry**.

○ A. yell   ○ B. happy   ○ C. sad   ○ D. tears

Explain how the analogy works: _____

_____

📖 Ready, Set, READ!

Read the folktale. Then answer the questions.

Shield and Spear   *A Chinese Folktale*

A merchant brought his shields and spears to market. He hung a banner to attract buyers. Soon onlookers gathered. The merchant held a shield above his head. He boasted, "Behold my shield! See its bold design! Notice its excellent quality, its perfect shape! No spear on earth can pierce it! My shield gives the safest protection! Buy one to become a respected warrior!"

The merchant put down the shield and picked up a spear. He raised it high above his head. He shouted, "Behold my spear of death! It is the sharpest spear on earth. My mighty spear can pierce any shield, no matter how hard, in one blow! Buy one to become a champion in battle!"

The merchant put down his spear, pleased with his speeches. A child came forward, saying, "Excuse me, sir. If I use your sharpest spear to strike your strongest shield, what will happen then?"

The merchant gulped. He opened his mouth but could find no answer. He rolled up his banner and left the market.

1. What is the job of a merchant?

   ○ A. joking   ○ B. selling   ○ C. fighting   ○ D. protecting

2. Why did the merchant suddenly leave?

   _____

   _____

๑ BrainTeaser ๑

Each word below is missing the same letter from its beginning and end. Complete every word using a *different* missing letter pair.

1. ____ ig ____

2. ____ omi ____

3. ____ oin ____

4. ____ ras ____

5. ____ abe ____

6. ____ azo ____

7. ____ rie ____

8. ____ earl ____

9. ____ ypis ____

Morning Jumpstarts: Reading, Grade 4 © 2013 Scholastic Teaching Resources

Name _____ Date _____

WORD of the Day

Use the word below in a sentence about a person who explored the unknown for the first time.

pioneer: (n.) *someone who goes first, explores the unknown, or leads the way so that others can follow*

_____

_____

Sentence Mender

Rewrite the sentence to make it correct.

Bruno which walks my dog also waters the plants

_____

Cursive Quote

Copy the quotation in cursive writing.

Fall seven times, stand up eight.

—Japanese proverb

- -

_____

- -

What does this proverb mean? Explain your idea in cursive on another sheet of paper.

Analogy of the Day

Complete the analogy.

Up is to **down** as _____ is to **fiction**.

○ A. fact   ○ B. book   ○ C. story   ○ D. figure

Explain how the analogy works: _____

_____

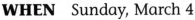

📖 Ready, Set, READ!

Read the invitation. Then answer the questions.

It's a Potluck Party!*

Do you have a sweet tooth?
Do you like to try all kinds of desserts?
Then come join our delicious dessert tasting!

WHEN Sunday, March 4
2:00 P.M. to 5:00 P.M. (Have lunch first!)
WHY Dad got a new job—hooray!!
WHO Friends & family; kids & adults (but no pets)
WHERE 96 Rosa Road, Apartment 4 (2nd floor)
RSVP Call or text Ruby at 555-0121

   * *Each guest or group: Please bring a dessert to share.*
   Choose whatever you like!
   It can be homemade or store-bought.
   It can be ordinary or outrageous.
   We'll provide drinks and a special treat.
   We'll have fruit and veggies for guests who don't want sweets.

---

1. What is the reason for the party? _____

   _____

2. Explain what "potluck" means in this situation. _____

   _____

➳ BrainTeaser ➶

An *anagram* is a new word made using all the
letters of another word. *Opt* is an anagram for *top*.

Make an anagram for each word.

---

1. rose ⇔ _____   5. trace ⇔ _____

2. slot ⇔ _____   6. alert ⇔ _____

3. gear ⇔ _____   7. pools ⇔ _____

4. flit ⇔ _____   8. trees ⇔ _____

Name _____ Date _____

Morning Jumpstarts: Reading, Grade 4 © 2013 Scholastic Teaching Resources

WORD of the Day

Use the word below in a sentence to describe a rough object.

coarse: (adj.) *rough in texture; harsh to the touch*

_____

_____

Sentence Mender

Rewrite the sentence to make it correct.

Tomorro we will be vizit a bakery

_____

Cursive Quote

Copy the quotation in cursive writing.

Try and fail, but don't fail to try.

—Stephen Kaggwa

. . . .

. . . .

. . . .

What does Kaggwa mean by this saying? Write your answer in cursive on another sheet of paper.

Analogy of the Day

Complete the analogy.

Number is to **eight** as _____ is to **sandwich**.

O A. sixteen   O B. ate   O C. eat   O D. food

Explain how the analogy works: _____

_____

📖 Ready, Set, READ!

Read the fable. Then answer the questions.

Lion and Rabbit   *An Indian Fable From the Panchatantra*

   Long ago, Lion ruled the jungle. He was vain and greedy. The other animals lived in fear. They decided that one animal per kind would offer itself to Lion every day. They hoped this would calm Lion so the others might live in peace. So the plan began.

   Soon a rabbit had to offer itself. The oldest, wisest rabbit came forward. She went quietly to meet her fate. When Rabbit reached Lion, he was both hungry and annoyed.

   Rabbit spoke softly. "Master, my kind walked me here. But another lion attacked us by surprise. He killed the other rabbits. I managed to escape with my life, which I now offer to you," she said. "But I think that other lion may challenge you."

   Lion growled in rage. "Show me this challenger!" he demanded. So Rabbit led Lion to a deep pool. She pointed to the "other" lion in the water. Lion roared and bared his fangs at that beast, who responded with equal anger. Lion dove into the pool to attack his rival, but drowned.

   MORAL: Intelligence can defeat might.

1. Which word means the same as *vain*?

   ○ A. strong   ○ B. proud   ○ C. lazy   ○ D. humble

2. What did Lion really see? _____

_____

🌀 BrainTeaser 🌀

The words in each group make a sentence, but only if you put them in order.
Start each sentence with a capital letter. Use an end mark.

1. yet eyes don't your open

_____

2. would a second like you helping

_____

3. of is June day first tomorrow the

_____

4. the salad table could to bring the you

_____

Morning Jumpstarts: Reading, Grade 4 © 2013 Scholastic Teaching Resources

Name _____ Date _____

WORD of the Day

Use the word below in a sentence about something you helped to grow or expand.

increase: (v.) *to make or become larger in size or greater in number; to add to; to make grow, swell, or expand*

_____

_____

Sentence Mender

Rewrite the sentence to make it correct.

Im reading the book lizzerd music by daniel pinkwater

_____

Cursive Quote

Copy the quotation in cursive writing.

A chattering bird builds no nest.

—African proverb

_____

_____

_____

Explain what you think this proverb means. Write your answer in cursive on another sheet of paper.

Analogy of the Day

Complete the analogy.

He is to **she** as _____ is to **here**.

O A. him   O B. there   O C. they   O D. their

Explain how the analogy works: _____

_____

 **JUMPSTART 6** **Side B**

 # Ready, Set, READ!

Read the passage. Then answer the questions.

The UN-Fish

Tube feet

The creature most people call a starfish is misnamed. Its official scientific name is the sea star. Let's discover how sea stars differ from actual fish.

- Fish are vertebrates; they have backbones. Sea stars are invertebrates because they have no backbone. Their nearest relatives are other invertebrates: sea urchins, sea cucumbers, and sand dollars.

- Fish swim but can't walk. Sea stars walk but can't swim. Sea stars crawl on tiny tube feet, which grow on the underside of each arm. Tube feet end in stretchy suckers.

- Fish get oxygen as water moves through their gills. Sea stars get oxygen from the water their tube feet suck in!

- Fish have one stomach; sea stars have two. One stomach always stays in the body to digest food. The other acts as a traveling mouth. It comes out of the sea star's body to wrap around food the sea star traps with its tube feet. It takes that food back to the inside stomach for digesting.

1. Why is a sea star *not* a fish?
   - O A. It is too slow.
   - O B. It has tube feet.
   - O C. It needs oxygen.
   - O D. It has no backbone.

2. Which is *not* a job of tube feet?
   - O A. sucking
   - O B. crawling
   - O C. digesting
   - O D. trapping

⑨ BrainTeaser ⑥

Onomatopoeia is a word that sounds like what it means. Examples are *buzz*, *hiss*, and *oink*.

Finish each simple sentence with onomatopoeia.

1. Soda cans _____ .

2. A wood fire _____ .

3. Leaves _____ .

4. Water balloons _____ .

5. Heavy chains _____ .

20

Name _____ Date _____

WORD of the Day

Use the word below in a sentence predicting something you might be doing ten years from now.

decade: (n.) *a period of ten years*

_____

_____

Sentence Mender

Rewrite the sentence to make it correct.

Turn up the heat cuz it is to cold in hear

_____

Cursive Quote

Copy the quotation in cursive writing.

Whatever you are, be a good one.

—Abraham Lincoln

_____

_____

_____

_____

How can any person make this goal come true? Write your answer in cursive on another sheet of paper.

Analogy of the Day

Complete the analogy.

Toe is to **foot** as _____ is to **face**.

○ A. finger   ○ B. nose   ○ C. head   ○ D. knee

Explain how the analogy works: _____

_____

Morning Jumpstarts: Reading, Grade 4 © 2013 Scholastic Teaching Resources

 **Side B**

Ready, Set, READ!

Read the poem.
Then answer the questions.

Caterpillar

Little Isabella Miller
Had a fuzzy caterpillar.
First it crawled upon her mother,
Then upon her baby brother.
They said, "Isabella Miller!
Put away your caterpillar!"

Little Isabella Miller
Had a fuzzy caterpillar.
First it crawled upon her brother,
Then upon her great-grandmother.
Gran said, "Isabella Miller,
How I love your caterpillar!"

1. How are the two verses alike?

_____

_____

_____

_____

_____

2. How do the two verses differ?

_____

_____

_____

_____

_____

3. Which person in Isabella's family liked her

caterpillar most? _____

_____

⑨ BrainTeaser ⑥

Complete each saying below using a word from the word bank.

1. Actions speak louder than _____ .

2. All that glitters is not _____ .

3. Don't put all your eggs in one _____ .

4. Honesty is the best _____ .

5. Look before you _____ .

6. Practice makes _____ .

7. The early bird gets the _____ .

8. You can't teach an old dog new _____ .

Word Bank

gold
leap
tricks
worm
words
policy
basket
perfect

22

Name _____ Date _____

WORD of the Day

Use the word below in a sentence that suggests why people fear toxic waste dumps.

toxic: (adj.) *poisonous, deadly*

_____

_____

Sentence Mender

Rewrite the sentence to make it correct.

The older childrins can make there own lunchs

_____

Cursive Quote

Copy the quotation in cursive writing.

Repetition is the mother of learning.

—White Mountain Apache saying

_____

_____

_____

Do you agree with this idea? Explain your answer in cursive on another sheet of paper.

Analogy of the Day

Complete the analogy.

Desk is to **classroom** as _____ is to **solar system.**

O A. school   O B. student   O C. universe   O D. planet

Explain how the analogy works: _____

_____

Morning Jumpstarts: Reading, Grade 4 © 2013 Scholastic Teaching Resources

 # Ready, Set, READ!

Read the dictionary entry.
Then answer the questions.

beam (beem)

1. noun A ray or band of light from a flashlight, a car headlight, or the sun.

2. noun A long, thick piece of wood, concrete, or metal used to support the roof or floors of a building.

3. verb To shine. *The sun beamed across the water.*

4. verb To smile widely. *Greg beamed when he saw the "A" on his report.*

***verb* beaming, beamed**

1. Which meaning of **beam** fits when you are very happy?

_____

2. Write a sentence that uses **beam** as a noun.

_____

_____

_____

_____

_____

☾ BrainTeaser ☾

Hink Pinks are one-syllable word pairs that rhyme to fit clues.
Solve these Hink Pink riddles.

Example

angry father = mad dad

1. What is the label on a paper sack? _____

2. Where do Mickey and Minnie live? _____

3. Where is a cozy place to read? _____

4. Who is the best collector of postage? _____

5. What are unusual coins given back? _____

6. What is a shabby trumpet? _____

Morning Jumpstarts: Reading, Grade 4 © 2013 Scholastic Teaching Resources

Name _____ Date _____

WORD of the Day

Use the word below in a sentence that tells about how a well-trained service dog can help someone in need.

assist: (v.) *to help or aid*

_____

_____

Sentence Mender

Rewrite the sentence to make it correct.

Jason asked can you help me find my keys

_____

_____

Cursive Quote

Copy the quotation in cursive writing.

We read to know we are not alone.

—C.S. Lewis

_____

- -

_____

_____

How can reading affect a person's mood? Explain in cursive on another sheet of paper.

Analogy of the Day

Complete the analogy.

Warm is to **hot** as _____ is to **cold**.

○ A. hot   ○ B. cool   ○ C. ice   ○ D. humid

Explain how the analogy works: _____

_____

📖 Ready, Set, READ!

Read the story. Then answer the questions.

Stay Near

When Scott hiked the mountains, his dog Bailey always came along. "Stay near," Scott would command, and Bailey always did. Well, almost always.

They were high on their favorite trail one day. Near dusk, Scott stopped to rest before descending. At that moment Bailey spotted a rabbit—and off he dashed. Scott shouted, "Bailey! Stay near!" He sprinted after his dog, repeating the command. He ran and shouted until he was out of breath, but Bailey was out of sight.

It was now fully dark. Scott phoned a friend to report that he would stay on the mountain all night; he would never abandon Bailey. Scott built a fire. He hollered for Bailey until his throat ached. Hours passed and still no dog. Finally, Scott fell asleep, feeling gloomy and scared. He dreamed of the beach, of surf tickling his toes. A huge wave washed over his face, waking him with a start. Bailey was licking his cheek.

1. What does *descending* mean?

   ○ A. relaxing   ○ B. daydreaming   ○ C. climbing   ○ D. going down

2. Why did Scott call a friend? _____

   _____

⑨ BrainTeaser ⑥

Hinky Pinkies are two-syllable word pairs that rhyme to fit clues.
Solve these Hinky Pinky riddles.

Example

arctic tooth = polar molar

1. What is a clever cat? _____

2. What is a box for huge rocks? _____

3. What is knitwear for a baby cat paw? _____

4. What is odder trouble? _____

5. What is a soft shaky tummy? _____

6. What is a fortunate swimming bird? _____

Name _____ Date _____

WORD of the Day

Use the word below in a sentence to describe something you do in a careless hurry.

haste: (n) *the act of hurrying; careless rushing*

_____

_____

Sentence Mender

Rewrite the sentence to make it correct.

The science teach gives we short quizs every days

_____

Cursive Quote

Copy the quotation in cursive writing.

Let your conscience be your guide.

—Jiminy Cricket (cartoon character)

_____

_____

_____

_____

How does your conscience guide you? Write your answer in cursive on another sheet of paper.

Analogy of the Day

Complete the analogy.

Whimper is to **cry** as _____ is to **laugh**.

○ A. laughter   ○ B. timid   ○ C. giggle   ○ D. funny

Explain how the analogy works: _____

_____

📖 Ready, Set, READ!

Read the passage. Then answer the questions.

Geographic Center of United States

It's pretty easy to find the center of a circle. A circle is a *regular* figure. Every point around the edge is as far from the center as every other. If you put a pin in that center, the circle would balance.

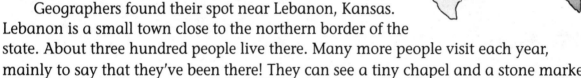

It's harder to find the center of an *irregular* figure. Picture the United States—leaving out Alaska and Hawaii. Our nation has a center. But where?

The best answer is an estimate. Geographers have made a fairly close one. They pictured the "lower 48" as one mass. Then they used advanced math. They figured out the point where this mass would balance.

Geographers found their spot near Lebanon, Kansas. Lebanon is a small town close to the northern border of the state. About three hundred people live there. Many more people visit each year, mainly to say that they've been there! They can see a tiny chapel and a stone marker.

1. What makes it harder to find the center of an irregular figure than of a regular one?

_____

_____

2. Why do you think geographers left out Alaska and Hawaii in their work?

_____

_____

🌀BrainTeaser🌀

Unscramble each dance word.
Write it correctly in the spaces.
Then unscramble the boxed letters
to name another dance word.

_____

KALOP □ ___ ___ ___ □

SWITT ___ ___ ___ ___ □

ANGOT ___ ___ □ ___ ___

TELLBA ___ ___ ___ □ ___ ___

LOBORE ___ ___ ___ ___ □ ___

ERLE □ ___ ___ ___

Morning Jumpstarts: Reading, Grade 4 © 2013 Scholastic Teaching Resources

Name _____ Date _____

WORD of the Day

Use the word below in a sentence about a mountain range.

jagged: (adj.) *having a ragged or uneven edge with many sharp high points and deep notches*

_____

_____

Sentence Mender

Rewrite the sentence to make it correct.

How many legs does spiders has

_____

Cursive Quote

Copy the quotation in cursive writing.

If you can read this, thank a teacher.

—Anonymous

- -

- -

- -

How does reading help you in your life? Explain in cursive on another sheet of paper.

Analogy of the Day

Complete the analogy.

Rooster is to **crow** as _____ is to **neigh**.

○ A. horse   ○ B. chicken   ○ C. purr   ○ D. agree

Explain how the analogy works: _____

_____

📖 Ready, Set, READ!

Read the passage. Then answer the questions.

Why Opossum Has a Bare Tail   *A Creek/Muscogee Tale of Tails*

One night, Opossum spied his friend Raccoon. Opossum had always loved Raccoon's bushy tail with many rings. So Opossum asked, "Raccoon, how did you get those rings?"

Raccoon proudly stroked his tail and answered, "I created them myself. First I wrapped strips of bark around my tail here and here and here," he pointed. "Then I held my tail over a fire. The uncovered fur turned black. But the fur under the bark stayed light, as you see. Lovely, isn't it?"

Opossum thanked Raccoon and scuttled away. First he built a fire. Next he wrapped bark strips around his furry tail. Then he stuck his tail right into the flame. Opossum instantly scorched off all his tail hair. The tail became bare.

Opossum wailed about his naked tail. All he could do was wait for new fur to grow back. And wait he did. But Opossum's tail was so badly burned that the fur never grew back. Opossum's tail remained bare for his entire life. And so it's been for opossums ever since.

1. Which word best describes Opossum?
    ○ A. naked   ○ B. patient   ○ C. envious   ○ D. curious

2. What kind of text is this?
    ○ A. nonfiction   ○ B. legend   ○ C. poetry   ○ D. drama

🌀 BrainTeaser 🌀

Write a synonym from the word bank for each boldface word below.

Word Bank

first
plain
tremble
concern
childish
supporter

1. **Humble** home _____

2. Team **sponsor** _____

3. **Initial** report _____

4. Mice **quiver** _____

5. Shows **courtesy** _____

6. **Juvenile** behavior _____

Morning Jumpstarts: Reading, Grade 4 © 2013 Scholastic Teaching Resources

Name _____ Date _____

WORD of the Day

Use the word below in a sentence about separating a play area.

enclose: (v.) *to shut something in on all sides, surround*

_____

_____

Sentence Mender

Rewrite the sentence to make it correct.

They taken the bus to see there grandmother in kansas.

_____

Cursive Quote

Copy the quotation in cursive writing.

Prepare the umbrella before it rains.

—Malay proverb

What advice does this saying offer? Write your answer in cursive on another sheet of paper.

Analogy of the Day

Complete the analogy.

Orange is to **fruit** as _____ is to **vehicle**.

O A. car   O B. vegetable   O C. yellow   O D. driver

Explain how the analogy works: _____

_____

 # Ready, Set, READ!

Read the passage. Then answer the questions.

Making a Difference

It probably cheers you up to receive a card you didn't expect. Hannah Newton surely thought so. She was only seven, but she understood the joy that a happy surprise can bring.

Hannah turned this idea into an outreach project to help others. She thought it would be kind to send surprise cards to needy people. But she knew she couldn't do it alone. So she visited classrooms all over her area. She asked other kids to join her. Together they made cards with hopeful messages inside. She gathered over 800 surprise cards for people who needed a boost. Adults helped her deliver the cards wherever they could do the most good.

Hannah's idea has become the *Children Who Care Club*. Kids make cards each month to cheer up the homeless, the elderly, and the sick. She says, "Even though my age is small, my heart is big!"

1. What gave Hannah her idea to help others?

_____

_____

_____

_____

_____

2. Why might some elderly people need cheering up?

_____

_____

_____

_____

_____

⊙ BrainTeaser ⊙

The word bank lists pioneer words. Each word is hidden in the puzzle. Find and circle each word.

Word Bank

BONNET	PIONEER
BUFFALO	PRAIRIE
CORNMEAL	QUILT
HARDSHIP	RUMBLE
HOMESTEAD	SCOUT
HUNGER	SUPPLIES
ILLNESS	TRADERS
JOURNALS	TRAIL
LANTERN	WAGON
NAVIGATE	YOKE

```
I L L N E S S R Y B H P O S
T R A I L Y W D N U O I T K
C O R N M E A L A F M O R R
R M C I S B E N V F E N A E
U P L C O I R R I A S E D G
K K O N R E U N G L T E E N
N U N I T M U T A O E R R U
T E A N B F Y P T K A E S H
T R A L D N A I E A D D V Y
P L E S L A N R U O J J S O
P I H S D R A H W A G O N K
S U P P L I E S T L I U Q E
```

Morning Jumpstarts: Reading, Grade 4 © 2013 Scholastic Teaching Resources

Name _____   Date _____

WORD of the Day

Use the word below in a sentence that tells about your favorite part of a movie, book, or TV show.

portion: (n.) *a part, or a share of something*

_____

_____

Sentence Mender

Rewrite the sentence to make it correct.

Would you likes budder or sour crime on you bake potato

_____

Cursive Quote

Copy the quotation in cursive writing.

There is no substitute for hard work.

—Thomas A. Edison

_____

_____

_____

_____

Do you think that Edison was right? Write your answer in cursive on another sheet of paper.

Analogy of the Day

Complete the analogy.

Skyscraper is to **tall** as _____ is to **sweet**.

○ A. pool   ○ B. sugary   ○ C. apartment   ○ D. candy

Explain how the analogy works: _____

_____

📖 Ready, Set, READ!

Haiku is a form of poetry. It is often about nature, and it rarely rhymes. Haiku poets try to create one sharp image in very few words.

Read the haiku. Then answer the questions.

Four Haiku From Japan

For this lovely bowl
Let us arrange some flowers
Since there is no rice . . .
by Basho

Oh! I ate them all
And oh! What a stomach-ache . . .
Green stolen apples
by Shiki

Windy winter rain . . .
My silly big umbrella
Tries walking backward
by Shisei-Jo

You stupid scarecrow!
Under your very stick-feet
Birds are stealing beans!
by Yayu

1. Which word best describes the feeling in Yayu's haiku?
   ○ A. annoyance
   ○ B. ignorance
   ○ C. pleasure
   ○ D. curiosity

2. Basho suggests arranging flowers in the lovely bowl to
   ○ A. have a project.
   ○ B. decorate his home.
   ○ C. cover up rice stains.
   ○ D. avoid thinking of hunger.

3. Describe how Shisei-Jo's umbrella looks. _____

_____

⊚ BrainTeaser ⊚

Write the words from the word bank in alphabetical order in the rows of the grid. Circle the column that has another word for *speak*.

Word Bank

PEARL   CLOUD   HOSTS
KNEEL   FLUTE

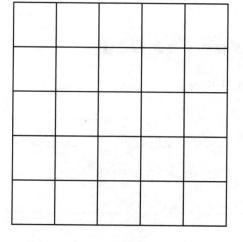

Morning Jumpstarts: Reading, Grade 4 © 2013 Scholastic Teaching Resources

Name _____ Date _____

WORD of the Day

Use the word below in a sentence about something unusual that you have seen, tasted, heard, or done.

unique: (adj.) *one of a kind; rare, unusual, remarkable*

_____

_____

Sentence Mender

Rewrite the sentence to make it correct.

we muss start on time to finishing the game by dark

_____

Cursive Quote

Copy the quotation in cursive writing.

It's kind of fun to do the impossible.

—Walt Disney

- -

- -

- -

What can Disney mean by these words? Write your answer in cursive on another sheet of paper.

Analogy of the Day

Complete the analogy.

Piano is to **musician** as _____ is to **scientist**.

○ A. discovery   ○ B. microscope   ○ C. guitar   ○ D. glasses

Explain how the analogy works: _____

_____

Morning Jumpstarts: Reading, Grade 4 © 2013 Scholastic Teaching Resources

 # Ready, Set, READ!

Read the passage. Then answer the questions.

Building an Igloo

An igloo is a dome-shaped hut made of blocks of hard snow. It has no corners. Inuit builders can make an igloo in about an hour. They work from the inside up. Here's how:

1. Pick a spot. Cut large blocks of icy snow. Make them about 3 feet wide, 2 feet tall, and 6 inches thick.

2. Stand in the hole left behind when you cut the blocks. Make a block circle around that hole. Tip each block inward a bit.

3. Now slice the tops off the first layer of blocks to start a big spiral. The lowest point meets the ground. The highest point is a full block tall.

4. Now add more blocks, starting from the lowest point. Spiral the blocks upward, and tip each block inward a bit. Keep spiraling around until the dome is almost closed.

5. Close the hole at the top by cutting a block to fit. Then chop out a door at the ground. Make it only as big as needed to crawl in and out.

1. How is an igloo different from other huts? _____
_____
_____
_____

2. Explain how the spiral helps shape the igloo and keep it standing.

_____
_____
_____
_____
_____

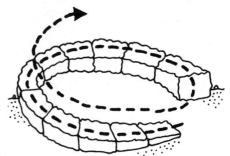

☺ BrainTeaser ☺

Find the extra word in each sentence and cross it out.

1. How many more chances do not we get?

2. Let's meet after school lets ends tomorrow.

3. This table spoon needs to be set for six people.

4. The noisy garbage bag truck woke me up at dawn.

5. Remember to take home your empty lunch money box.

36

Name _____ Date _____

WORD of the Day

Use the word below in a sentence about taking a photograph.

focus: (v.) *to adjust to create a clear image; to direct or fix on something*

_____

_____

Sentence Mender

Rewrite the sentence to make it correct.

Oh my goodness we won the raffle

_____

Cursive Quote

Copy the quotation in cursive writing.

Always be a little kinder than necessary.

—James M. Barrie

_____

_____

_____

_____

What does this saying tell you about Barrie? Write your answer in cursive on another sheet of paper.

Analogy of the Day

Complete the analogy.

Cheerful is to **glad** as _____ is to **below**.

○ A. under   ○ B. above   ○ C. water   ○ D. thrilled

Explain how the analogy works: _____

_____

 # Ready, Set, READ!

Read the story. Then answer the questions.

Growing Pains

"Some dragon I am!" whined Valo. "All the other dragons breathe fire whenever they want. Some emit clouds of foul-smelling gas. But all I can manage is a cough."

"Valo, my scaly darling, you're still young," soothed his mother. "Your fire glands aren't mature enough. Have patience."

Valo had heard this explanation before, but he was weary of waiting. So he stomped around, hoping to speed up his growth. He rehearsed his roar, which was still peepy. He thrashed his tail in mock fury, splintering a few trees. He flew a bit and bashed some boulders, but no smoke, fire, or gas.

Valo came to a pasture of red peppers, the same color as his glowing eyes. In boredom, he nibbled a few of them. They were fiery hot peppers, which blistered his throat and made him gasp. The sting thrilled him, so he gorged himself on the whole crop! He ate so fast that he had to burp. When he did, an explosion of orange fire and rank air burst forth.

1. What is Valo's problem?

_____

_____

_____

_____

_____

2. How does his mother try to calm him?

_____

_____

_____

_____

3. What kind of text is this?
   - A. journal
   - B. fantasy
   - C. history
   - D. myth

⊚ BrainTeaser ⊚

Write *a, e, i, o, u,* or *y* to finish spelling each instrument.

1. fl ____ t ____

2. h ____ rp

3. dr ____ ms

4. tr ____ mp ____ t

5. b ____ gp ____ p ____ s

6. tr ____ mb ____ n ____

7. ____ rg ____ n

8. r ____ c ____ rd ____ r

9. g ____ ____ t ____ r

10. t ____ mb ____ ____ r ____ n ____

Morning Jumpstarts: Reading, Grade 4 © 2013 Scholastic Teaching Resources

Name _____ Date _____

WORD of the Day

Use the word below in a sentence about an ancient clay bowl.

artifact: (n.) *an object made by humans long ago, often a tool, ornament, or household item*

_____

_____

Sentence Mender

Rewrite the sentence to make it correct.

Keep all knifes away from small childs?

_____

Cursive Quote

Copy the quotation in cursive writing.

Play is not a luxury. Play is a necessity.

—Kay Redfield Jamison

_____

_____

_____

What do you think makes play so necessary? Write your answer in cursive on another sheet of paper.

Analogy of the Day

Complete the analogy.

Page is to **book** as _____ is to **pencil**.

○ A. pen   ○ B. write   ○ C. desk   ○ D. eraser

Explain how the analogy works: _____

_____

📖 Ready, Set, READ!

Read the interview. Then answer the questions.

Sub Grub   Dara interviews Jorge, U.S. Navy Culinary Specialist

Dara: *What exactly is a Culinary Specialist?*

Jorge: I'm a cook! On a submarine, like anywhere, people have to eat. But we can't just call in pizza!

Dara: *How's the food on submarines?*

Jorge: It's the best the Navy has to offer! Great food is our reward for all our sacrifices. We give up windows, fresh air, land, and space for months.

Dara: *What do you do besides cook?*

Jorge: Anything else the sub needs, and everything about food. The hardest part for a CS is the advance planning. I shop for three months of food, four meals a day, for the whole crew. Menus must be balanced, healthy, and not boring. Space is so tight that storage is a challenge, too.

Dara: *What foods are the crew's favorites?*

Jorge: Steak, lobster, and ice cream! We have a soft-serve ice cream machine, but it's not just for fun. Ice cream has calcium, eggs, and fruit.

1. What does CS stand for?
   - ○ A. Crew Status
   - ○ B. Calcium Service
   - ○ C. Cook Sub
   - ○ D. Culinary Specialist

2. Why does the Navy provide such great food for a submarine?

   _____

   _____

   _____

   _____

   _____

   _____

🌀 BrainTeaser 🌀

Complete the category chart. The letters above each column tell the first letter for each word. One word is done for you.

	B	E	S	T
Names of Cities		El Paso		
Map Words				
Forest Things				
Kitchen Things				

Name _____ Date _____

WORD of the Day

Use the word below in a sentence describing a fancy event.

lavish: (adj.) *far more than enough; beyond what is needed or expected; overly generous*

_____

_____

Sentence Mender

Rewrite the sentence to make it correct.

How do you say the word for homework? in spanish asked betsy.

_____

Cursive Quote

Copy the quotation in cursive writing.

You have to leave room in life to dream.

—Buffy Sainte-Marie

_____

_____

_____

What makes dreaming worth your time? Explain your answer in cursive on another sheet of paper.

Analogy of the Day

Complete the analogy.

Teacher is to **faculty** as _____ is to **chorus**.

○ A. school   ○ B. night   ○ C. choir   ○ D. soprano

Explain how the analogy works: _____

_____

Morning Jumpstarts: Reading, Grade 4 © 2013 Scholastic Teaching Resources

📖 Ready, Set, READ!

A *proverb* is a wise saying.

Read the proverbs below, which warn of rain. Then answer the questions.

Will It Rain?

- Red sky in morning—sailors, take warning!
  Red sky at night—sailor's delight.

- Thunder in morn, all day storm;
  Thunder at night, traveler's delight.

- Catchy drawer and sticky door:
  Coming rain will pour and pour.

- A ring around the sun or moon
  Means rain or snow is coming soon.

- If grass is dry at morning light
  Look for rain before the night.

- Ants that move their eggs and climb
  Tell rain is coming anytime.

- When clouds look like smoke
  A wise man wears his cloak.

1. What features do all these proverbs share?

   _____

   _____

   _____

   _____

2. Which proverb sounds most logical to you? Explain.

   _____

   _____

   _____

   _____

   _____

   _____

⦿ BrainTeaser ⦿

Each sentence below has two blanks. Both use the same letters to form different three-letter words. Fill them in. The first one is done for you.

1. My _____ear_____ still hurts but my eyes _____are_____ fine.

2. _____ can we figure out _____ left the message?

3. After the storm, we _____ that there _____ a rainbow!

4. They _____ the first game, but who is ahead _____?

5. I am _____ sure how many pounds equal one _____.

6. Water ran into the _____, _____ the drain was open!

Morning Jumpstarts: Reading, Grade 4 © 2013 Scholastic Teaching Resources

JUMPSTART 18

Name _____ Date _____

WORD of the Day

Use the word below in a sentence about a fair exchange you might make with a friend.

barter: (v.) *to trade objects or food for goods or services without using money; exchange*

_____

_____

Sentence Mender

Rewrite the sentence to make it correct.

Mom like chocolate covered cherrys better of all candy

_____

Cursive Quote

Copy the quotation in cursive writing.

A joy that's shared is a joy made double.

—Anonymous

- -

- -

- -

How can sharing spread more joy? Write your answer in cursive on another sheet of paper.

Analogy of the Day

Complete the analogy.

Lantern is to **light** as _____ is to **dig**.

○ A. bulb   ○ B. shovel   ○ C. hole   ○ D. rake

Explain how the analogy works: _____

_____

📖 Ready, Set, READ!

Read the passage. Then answer the questions.

Natural Pigment

The human eye can see millions of colors. Color pleases us and varies our world. Every culture uses color: people paint their skin, dye cloth, brighten up their homes, and make art.

Most natural materials have *pigment*—something in them that contains color. Did you ever get grass stains on your clothes? It came from pigment in the grass rubbing off on you. The first dyes may have been found by accidents just like that. Early people might have stained their skin or clothes with rock dust, food, or crushed plants. Over time, they learned to make dyes from nature's pigments. An important example of this is *cochineal*.

Grinding cochineal between stones

Cochineal comes from the crushed bodies of a beetle found in the Americas. Aztec and Mayan people would collect the beetles, drown them in hot water, dry them in the sun, and then crush them into a powder. Then they made the powder into a paste that could give yarn or cloth a deep red color. The powder has the same name as the insect it came from.

1. What is pigment? _____

_____

2. Cochineal is a kind of
   ○ A. culture   ○ B. plant   ○ C. cloth   ○ D. insect

🌀 BrainTeaser 🌀

Write all the different words you can spell using three or more letters from the word *conversation*.

_____

_____

_____

_____

Morning Jumpstarts: Reading, Grade 4 © 2013 Scholastic Teaching Resources

Name _____   Date _____

WORD of the Day

Use the word below in a sentence about an example of this kind of writing that you enjoy reading.

prose: (n.) *ordinary style of text; writing that is not poetry*

_____

_____

Sentence Mender

Rewrite the sentence to make it correct.

Do you thought their will be a fire drill today!

_____

Cursive Quote

Copy the quotation in cursive writing.

Teach us to give and not to count the cost.

—Ignatius Loyola

How can there be different kinds of giving? Explain your idea in cursive on another sheet of paper.

Analogy of the Day

Complete the analogy.

Straw is to **drink** as _____ is to **reach**.

○ A. shelf   ○ B. milk   ○ C. ladder   ○ D. cup

Explain how the analogy works: _____

_____

📖 Ready, Set, READ!

Read the myth. Then answer the questions.

The Spirit Dog   *A Cherokee Myth*

The Cherokee depended on corn for food. They pounded it into meal for bread and mush. They stored it in large baskets.

At dawn one day, a woman went to her basket for cornmeal. She found a great mess. She noticed huge dog prints in the scattered cornmeal. They came from no ordinary dog. So she ran to the village and called the people together. She warned that a visit from a spirit dog was a bad sign. So the people agreed to scare the spirit dog so badly that it would never return.

That night everyone brought drums and rattles. They hid by the cornmeal and waited. Soon came a loud flapping sound. Looking up, they saw a huge dog flying in. It knocked over the baskets to get cornmeal. Just then, the people jumped up, beating drums and shaking rattles like thunder. The spirit dog ran off as the people and noise chased him.

At the top of a hill, the spirit dog leaped into the sky and flew into the darkness. Cornmeal fell from its mouth to form a faint path. Bits of cornmeal soon turned into stars.

1. What bad things might have happened if the spirit dog kept coming?

_____

_____

2. Many cultures have another name for the faint path the spirit dog made in the sky. Which name do you think it has in English?

   ○ A. Milky Way   ○ B. Great Dog   ○ C. Big Dipper   ○ D. Flying Fish

☺ BrainTeaser ☺

Each word below is missing the same letter from its beginning and end.
Complete every word using a *different* missing letter pair.

1. ____ indo ____

2. ____ noc ____

3. ____ an ____

4. ____ dg ____

5. ____ rus ____

6. ____ oya ____

7. ____ lum ____

8. ____ ealt ____

9. ____ ooste ____

Name _____ Date _____

Use the word below in a sentence about a sporting event or a debate.

agile: (adj.) *able to move quickly and easily; nimble; swift*

_____

_____

Sentence Mender

Rewrite the sentence to make it correct.

He watch in horror as a green snake creeped tword the tent

_____

Cursive Quote

Copy the quotation in cursive writing.

Reading is a discount ticket to everywhere.

—Mary Schmich

_____

_____

_____

What does Schmich mean by this statement? Write your answer in cursive on another sheet of paper.

Analogy of the Day

Complete the analogy.

Coal is to **dark** as _____ is to **hard**.

O A. day   O B. floor   O C. soft   O D. sand

Explain how the analogy works: _____

_____

📖 Ready, Set, READ!

Read the story. Then answer the questions.

The Ant Farm

A student describes her science project in a speech to her class.

You've all seen my ant farm in the back of our classroom. This is how I made it, care for it, and feel about it.

I got the idea online. So first, I collected backyard ants in a jar. I gathered dry dirt in another jar. I got an old picture frame from my mom to use as the farm. I figured I could watch the ants at work through the glass.

I put the dirt and then ants in. Once they were inside, I fed the ants tiny bits of fruit, veggies, and bread crumbs. I've also been feeding them dead flies and moths. I give them liquid by soaking a cotton ball in sugar water.

Many of you thought my ant farm was dumb, even disgusting at first. But soon I saw you staring at it. You watched my ants dig tunnels. You watched me feed and care for them. This makes me proud and my ants famous.

1. What is an ant farm? _____

_____

2. How did the attitude of the classmates change?

_____

_____

☺ BrainTeaser ☺

Use the clues to complete a word that starts with *pre*.

1. Hunter's victim   PRE _____

2. Squish   PRE ____ ____

3. Attractive   PRE ____ ____ ____

4. Choose over another   PRE ____ ____ ____

5. Make believe   PRE ____ ____ ____ ____

6. Forecast what may come   PRE ____ ____ ____ ____

7. Salty snack food   PRE ____ ____ ____

Morning Jumpstarts: Reading, Grade 4 © 2013 Scholastic Teaching Resources

Name _____ Date _____

Morning Jumpstarts: Reading, Grade 4 © 2013 Scholastic Teaching Resources

WORD of the Day

Use the word below in a sentence about picking a team leader.

appoint: (v.) *to name to an office or position; officially choose or decide on*

_____

_____

Sentence Mender

Rewrite the sentence to make it correct.

be home bye for oclock said Dad

_____

Cursive Quote

Copy the quotation in cursive writing.

Champions keep playing until they get it right.

—Billie Jean King

_____

_____

_____

What do you think King, a tennis champion, means? Write your answer in cursive on another sheet of paper.

Analogy of the Day

Complete the analogy.

Carrot is to **vegetable** as _____ is to **planet**.

○ A. Mars   ○ B. sun   ○ C. corn   ○ D. galaxy

Explain how the analogy works: _____

_____

📖 Ready, Set, READ!

Read the passage. Then answer the questions.

Idaho Potatoes

We Idaho folk worship our potatoes. Idaho grows the biggest and finest ones anywhere. Out-of-staters can't believe it! A Utah cook once tried to buy a hundred pounds of potato from me, but I refused. "No, Ma'am!" I said. "I'd never sell just part of a potato. You buy a whole potato or none at all," I insisted.

Idaho potatoes are supremely tasty. They're the most buttery ones you'll ever eat. I suppose it's because we feed them like family: milk and cornmeal three times a day. Yeah, it must be that milk. Our potatoes are so creamy all you do is boil and mash them.

But Idaho potatoes aren't perfect. Our fields get so overcrowded you can hear grumbling from underground. "Roll over! You're squeezing me!" the 'taters complain. Then they poke up and cause problems on top. A guy I know got stuck for five hours under one pesky potato. His kids came looking for him when he didn't make it to supper. We all had to help drag him out.

1. What does the speaker suggest in his response to the Utah cook?

_____

_____

2. How does the picture support the speaker's claims?

_____

_____

❧ BrainTeaser ❧

Homophones are words that sound the same but have different spellings and meanings.

Write the correct word in each sentence.

1. Mom lets me _____ the turkey.   **baste** *or* **based**

2. Bears have thick, sharp _____.   **clause** *or* **claws**

3. Oh my, how tall they've _____!   **grown** *or* **groan**

4. Your library book is a week _____.   **overdo** *or* **overdue**

Morning Jumpstarts: Reading, Grade 4 © 2013 Scholastic Teaching Resources

Name _____ Date _____

WORD of the Day

Use the word below in a sentence to describe a key partner.

ally: (n.) *a person, group, or nation that agrees to support another to reach a shared goal; friend; partner*

_____

_____

Sentence Mender

Rewrite the sentence to make it correct.

The books silly titel make me laugh

_____

Cursive Quote

Copy the quotation in cursive writing.

It's not how big you are, it's how big you play.

—Anonymous

_____

- -

_____

What can it mean to "play big"? Write your answer in cursive on another sheet of paper.

Analogy of the Day

Complete the analogy.

Mine is to **yours** as _____ is to **hers**.

○ A. she   ○ B. him   ○ C. his   ○ D. he

Explain how the analogy works: _____

_____

📖 Ready, Set, READ!

Read the letter to the editor. Then answer the questions.

Dear Editor,

I read your newspaper sometimes. I like the section for suggesting ways to improve neighborhoods. People write about cleaning up parks, speeding up garbage pick-ups, improving mail delivery, and other subjects they think about. I'd like to add my two cents. My problem is with traffic lights.

I think the traffic lights on Central Avenue don't stay green long enough for the cross streets. My granddad walks me to school. We don't move so fast. If we don't start crossing Central just as the light turns green, we can barely get across in time. I don't think this is safe, and it's not fair. There are many older people and young kids where I live. We'd all benefit from longer light cycles. I think an extra 20 seconds of green would solve the problem.

Thank you for your attention.
Lynn Walker, age 8

1. What is the goal of Lynn's letter?
   - ○ A. to complain
   - ○ B. to add money
   - ○ C. to get published
   - ○ D. to adjust the light cycle

2. How would you describe her letter?
   - ○ A. angry
   - ○ B. lengthy
   - ○ C. helpful
   - ○ D. selfish

🌀 BrainTeaser 🌀

Unscramble each art word.
Write it correctly in the spaces.
Then unscramble the boxed letters to
name an art product made with egg.

_____

PLATES [ ] __ __ [ ] __

REAMF __ __ [ ] __

YCAL __ __ [ ] __

LEFT __ [ ] __ __

NAPIT __ __ __ [ ] __

ORANYC __ [ ] __ __ __ __

Morning Jumpstarts: Reading, Grade 4 © 2013 Scholastic Teaching Resources

Name _____ Date _____

WORD of the Day

Use the word below in a sentence that describes a photograph.

accurate: (adj.) *exactly right or correct; without error*

_____

_____

Sentence Mender

Rewrite the sentence to make it correct.

Strike tree yer out yelled the Umpire

_____

Cursive Quote

Copy the quotation in cursive writing.

A book is like a garden carried in the pocket.

—Chinese proverb

_____

_____

_____

_____

Why is a book compared to a garden? Explain your idea in cursive on another sheet of paper.

Analogy of the Day

Complete the analogy.

Sorry is to **regretful** as _____ is to **fragile**.

○ A. sturdy   ○ B. miserable   ○ C. lonely   ○ D. delicate

Explain how the analogy works: _____

_____

📖 Ready, Set, READ!

Read the letter. Then answer the questions.

23 April, 1846
Dearest Mother,

    How I yearn for you, James, wee Emma, and our agreeable farm! Eight long months have passed since I came here to Lowell. Every afternoon I propose to write. But each day's work at the mill tires me mightily.

    Share my thanks that I enjoy strong health. My wages bring in a decent three dollars per week. I share a modest room in a boarding house with five other girls. We are but ten minutes from the mill. Mrs. Howe provides a cold supper, though portions are woefully small.

    Our overseer is a stern leader. We must report to the loom by five each morning. It is often cold and dark at that tender hour, but no matter. Our day includes two half-hour meal breaks. We stop work by seven most evenings.

    I do not know when I shall visit. Perhaps for the turning of the new year? Winter travel may be hard, but I would endure a blizzard to see you all.

    From your most affectionate daughter,
             Mary

1. Why do you think Mary left home?

_____

_____

_____

_____

_____

2. What is Mary's living situation now?

_____

_____

_____

_____

_____

꒰ BrainTeaser ꒱

Write the words from the word bank in alphabetical order in the rows of the grid. Circle the column that has the name of a fictional character created by author Beverly Cleary.

Word Bank

TOWER   TEACH   TRULY
TITAN   THOSE

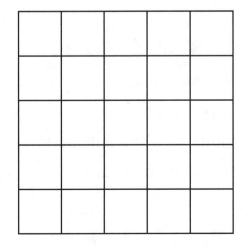

54

Name _____ Date _____

WORD of the Day

Use the word below in a sentence about an accident.

collide: (v.) *to crash or bump into; to strike, hit, or come together with force*

_____

_____

Sentence Mender

Rewrite the sentence to make it correct.

I knows all the words to all five verse's of This land is your land

_____

Cursive Quote

Copy the quotation in cursive writing.

When the mind is thinking, it is talking to itself.

—Plato

Do you agree with Plato? Explain. Write your answer in cursive on another sheet of paper.

Analogy of the Day

Complete the analogy.

Green is to **color** as _____ is to **spice.**

○ A. ketchup   ○ B. red   ○ C. cinnamon   ○ D. lemon

Explain how the analogy works: _____

_____

📖 Ready, Set, READ!

Read the recipe. Then answer the questions.

Whip up a dozen homemade soft pretzels!

Ingredients
$\frac{1}{3}$ cup baking soda
5 cups water
3 cups flour
1 teaspoon baking soda
$\frac{1}{4}$ cup honey
1 cup buttermilk
Coarse salt

Utensils
• Cookie sheet
• Cooking spray
• Measuring cups
• Non-aluminum cooking pot
• Pot holder
• Large mixing bowl and spoon

What to Do
1. Preheat oven to 400°F.
2. Grease cookie sheet with cooking spray.
3. Mix $\frac{1}{3}$ cup baking soda and water in pot. Boil, then let cool.
4. In bowl, blend flour and 1 tsp. baking soda. Add honey and buttermilk. Stir to form dough. Knead on a floured surface for 1 minute.
5. Divide dough into 12 equal pieces. Roll out each piece into a "snake" about 1 foot long. Twist into a pretzel knot. Pinch ends together.
6. Dip pretzels in baking soda water. Place on cookie sheet.
7. Sprinkle pretzels with salt. Bake until golden (about 10 minutes).

1. Why is baking soda listed twice?

_____

_____

_____

_____

2. What does it mean to *knead* dough? _____

_____

_____

_____

🌀 BrainTeaser 🌀

Write an antonym from the word bank for each boldface word below.

1. **Vacant** chair _____

2. **Previous** week _____

3. Plants **wither** _____

4. **Frantic** shoppers _____

5. **Sincere** smile _____

Word Bank

calm
false
blossom
occupied
following

Morning Jumpstarts: Reading, Grade 4 © 2013 Scholastic Teaching Resources

Name _____ Date _____

WORD of the Day

Use the word below in a sentence about lack of rain on a farm.

drought: (n.) *a long period of dry weather; extended time with little or no rain*

_____

_____

Sentence Mender

Rewrite the sentence to make it correct.

Arthur wynne make the 1st crossword puzzel in 1913

_____

Cursive Quote

Copy the quotation in cursive writing.

Once you learn to read, you will be forever free.

—Frederick Douglass

....

....

....

Douglass was born into slavery. Though it was against the law, he learned to read. How do those facts help explain the quotation? Respond in cursive on another sheet of paper.

Analogy of the Day

Complete the analogy.

Brake is to **stop** as _____ is to **cut**.

○ A. horn   ○ B. scissors   ○ C. slice   ○ D. tire

Explain how the analogy works: _____

_____

📖 Ready, Set, READ!

Read the lyrics. Then answer the questions.

My Grandfather's Clock *Traditional Folksong*

My grandfather's clock was too large for the shelf
So it stood ninety years on the floor.
It was taller by half than the old man himself
Though it weighed not a pennyweight more.
It was bought on the morn of the day that he was born
And was always his treasure and pride.
But it stopped short—never to go again—
When the old man died.

 Ninety years without slumbering (tick tock tick tock)
 His life's seconds numbering (tick tock tick tock)
 It stopped short—never to go again—
 When the old man died.

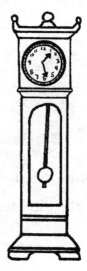

1. If the man was 6 feet tall, how tall was the clock? _____

_____

2. What was so remarkable about this clock? _____

_____

🌀 BrainTeaser 🌀

The word wheel holds nine letters. If you use all nine of them, you can form a nine-letter word about books. Form other words (from three to eight letters), always using the R in the center and any others.

_____

_____

_____

_____

Morning Jumpstarts: Reading, Grade 4 © 2013 Scholastic Teaching Resources

Name _____ Date _____

WORD of the Day

Use the word below in a sentence about an annoying sound.

constant: (adj.) *not stopping; always the same; unchanging*

_____

_____

Sentence Mender

Rewrite the sentence to make it correct.

Nineth president William henry Harrison serve for less then thirty-one day

_____

Cursive Quote

Copy the quotation in cursive writing.

One kind word can warm three winter months.

—Japanese saying

_____

_____

_____

What do you think this saying means? Write your answer in cursive on another sheet of paper.

Analogy of the Day

Complete the analogy.

Bottom is to **top** as _____ is to **left**.

○ A. leave   ○ B. up   ○ C. center   ○ D. right

Explain how the analogy works: _____

_____

📖 Ready, Set, READ!

Read the passage. Then answer the questions.

One of a Kind

Jim Abbot was an amazing athlete. His best sport was baseball. This lefty pitcher was a star in high school and in college. In 1987, he won the Sullivan Award as the nation's best amateur athlete. He pitched in the Olympics in 1988.

Abbot reached the major leagues in 1989. He won 87 games in his career. He even threw a no-hitter, which is rare for any pitcher.

When he pitched, Abbot did something other pitchers did not. He kept his glove tucked under his right arm. Once he released the ball, he slipped his hand into the glove to prepare to catch the ball if it came his way. If it did, he would catch it and quickly remove the ball from the glove in time to throw it. He did this smoothly and accurately.

Jim Abbot followed this routine with every pitch he made. Why? He did it because he had to. Abbot was born without a right hand.

1. Which word is the opposite of *amateur*?

○ A. adult　　○ B. professional　　○ C. beginner　　○ D. part-time

2. Why did Abbot pitch and field differently than other pitchers?

_____

_____

🌀 BrainTeaser 🌀

Use the clues to write a word that includes *z*.

1. Not hard working　　___ ___ Z ___

2. Feeling comfy and warm　　___ ___ Z ___

3. Flavorful and spicy　　Z ___ ___ ___ ___

4. Group of 12 things　　___ ___ Z ___ ___

5. Gentle wind　　___ ___ ___ ___ Z ___

6. Four-legged reptile　　___ ___ Z ___ ___ ___

Name _____ Date _____

WORD of the Day

Use the word below in a sentence about leaving a door open.

neglect: (v.) *to forget or give too little attention to*

_____

_____

Sentence Mender

Rewrite the sentence to make it correct.

My unkle always sing a dum song called the eggplant that ate chicago

_____

Cursive Quote

Copy the quotation in cursive writing.

You always pass failure on the way to success.

—Mickey Rooney

- -

- -

- -

How can failure now lead to success later? Explain your idea in cursive on another sheet of paper.

Analogy of the Day

Complete the analogy.

Simple is to **challenging** as _____ is to **create**.

○ A. easy   ○ B. destroy   ○ C. invest   ○ D. difficult

Explain how the analogy works: _____

_____

Ready, Set, READ!

Read the passage. Then answer the questions.

The Dog and His Reflection
by Aesop

A hungry dog was searching for a meal. Soon he came upon a sizable piece of meat. Overjoyed by his luck, he decided to carry the meat back to his den to eat in peace and comfort. On his way there, he loped proudly across a bridge over a stream. As he crossed, he looked down into the water. There he saw his own reflection. But the dog believed he was seeing another dog holding an even bigger piece of meat. His belly rumbled, but he paused to consider what to do.

He decided to steal the other dog's meat. But as he opened his mouth to do this, his own piece of meat fell. It splashed into the stream and was swept away. The dog lost his treasure and was left with only his hunger.

1. What does *overjoyed* mean?
   - ○ A. too happy
   - ○ B. unhappy
   - ○ C. happy again
   - ○ D. very happy

2. What lesson does this fable attempt to teach?

   _____

   _____

   _____

   _____

   _____

   _____

BrainTeaser

Write *a, e, i, o, u,* or *y* to finish spelling each baseball word.

1. ___ nn ___ ng

2. str ___ k ___

3. sl ___ gg ___ r

4. b ___ nt

5. gl ___ v ___

6. s ___ ngl ___

7. st ___ ___ l

8. tr ___ pl ___

9. m ___ ___ nd

10. f ___ ___ ld ___ r

11. t ___ g

12. sl ___ d ___

13. ___ ___ t

14. c ___ tch ___ r

62

Name _____ Date _____

WORD of the Day

Use the word below in a sentence about asking a favor.

response: (n.) *a reply; any answer given in words or by actions*

_____

_____

Sentence Mender

Rewrite the sentence to make it correct.

Jamille past the test and got the higher score of enybody

_____

Cursive Quote

Copy the quotation in cursive writing.

If we cannot be clever, we can always be kind.

—Alfred Fripp

_____

_____

_____

_____

Do you think that Fripp's words make sense? Explain your idea in cursive on another sheet of paper.

Analogy of the Day

Complete the analogy.

Wheel is to **bicycle** as _____ is to **pie**.

○ A. sweet   ○ B. fruit   ○ C. cake   ○ D. shape

Explain how the analogy works: _____

_____

📖 Ready, Set, READ!

Read the passage. Then answer the questions.

A Flood of Bats

Bracken Bat Cave is near San Antonio, Texas. It is the summer home to more than 20 million Mexican free-tailed bats. From March to October, Bracken holds one of the greatest mammal populations on earth.

Interested visitors can witness a Bracken Bat Flight. This outdoor event lasts between three and four hours. Keep these points in mind as you plan your visit:

- Bat Flights take place rain or shine. Dress for the weather and for rugged, dusty conditions near the cave.

- You may bring binoculars and cameras, but flash use is not allowed. You may not bring chairs, food, or pets.

- Bats are wild animals. They emerge nightly to hunt insects. But the exact time is unknown. It can take up to three hours for all bats to exit the cave.

- Bats are highly sensitive to noise. Remain as quiet as possible, and stay on the hillside near the cave.

1. What kind of animal is a bat?

   ○ A. reptile   ○ B. bird   ○ C. amphibian   ○ D. mammal

2. Which is *not* allowed at a Bracken Bat Flight?

   ○ A. feeding   ○ B. sleeping   ○ C. observing   ○ D. standing

⊚ BrainTeaser ⊚

What did the porcupine ask the cactus?

Solve each clue. Then copy each letter into its numbered box to find the answer to the riddle.

- Card game

  __ __ __ __ __
  2 6 11 7 8

- Pirate "yes"

  __ __ __
  1 4 3

- Cow sound

  __ __ __
  9 5 10

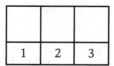

1	2	3

4	5	6

7	8

| 9 | 10 | 11 | **?**
|---|---|---|

Morning Jumpstarts: Reading, Grade 4 © 2013 Scholastic Teaching Resources

Name _____ Date _____

WORD of the Day

Use the word below in a sentence about a yearly event you enjoy.

annual: (adj.) *happening or coming once a year*

_____

_____

Sentence Mender

Rewrite the sentence to make it correct.

Wear were you on Saturday june 16 2012 dr miller?

_____

Cursive Quote

Copy the quotation in cursive writing.

I learned the value of hard work by working hard.

—Margaret Mead

_____

_____

_____

Why do so many successful people praise hard work? Write your answer in cursive on another sheet of paper.

Analogy of the Day

Complete the analogy.

Cracker is to **crispy** as _____ is to **gritty**.

○ A. sand ○ B. cookie ○ C. creamy ○ D. gravy

Explain how the analogy works: _____

_____

📖 Ready, Set, READ!

Read the passage. Then answer the questions.

Man and Dog

A man and his dog enter a diner and sit at the counter. The man tells the server that his dog can talk. "No way," the server replies.

"Way," the man answers. "Just listen!" He asks his dog to say what is atop every house.

"Roof," the dog barks. The server is unimpressed. So the man asks his dog another question.

"How does sandpaper feel?"

"Ruff," the dog barks. Still the server is unconvinced.

"Come on," she says. "Your dog can't talk any more than mine can."

"Usually you can't shut her up," the man insists. "Let me try again." Turning to his dog, he asks, "Molly, who is the best ball player ever?"

"Roof," answers Molly, wagging her tail in triumph. The server turns away, shaking her head. The man and the dog leave. Outside, Molly taps her owner with her large paw and asks, "Should I have said *Babe* Roof?"

1. What is the dog's name? _____

2. What makes this joke funny? _____

_____

⑨ BrainTeaser ⑥

Think of one word that all three words on the left have in common.
Write it on the line. The first one is done for you.

1. wagon
   cart   wheel _____
   Ferris

2. tree
   circus   _____
   diamond

3. spider
   world-wide   _____
   Charlotte's

4. picnic
   waste   _____
   Easter

5. baby
   olive   _____
   engine

6. pig
   ball-point   _____
   fountain

66

Morning Jumpstarts: Reading, Grade 4 © 2013 Scholastic Teaching Resources

Name _____ Date _____

Use the word below in a sentence to tell why you do not support a certain rule or plan.

oppose: (v.) *to be or act against something; fight or resist*

_____

_____

Sentence Mender

Rewrite the sentence to make it correct.

Can you belive that alaska has a town called y?

_____

Cursive Quote

Copy the quotation in cursive writing.

Don't look where you fall, but where you slipped.

—African proverb

_____

_____

_____

_____

What is the meaning of this proverb? Write your answer in cursive on another sheet of paper.

Analogy of the Day

Complete the analogy.

Driver is to **car** as _____ is to **train**.

○ A. pilot   ○ B. caboose   ○ C. track   ○ D. engineer

Explain how the analogy works: _____

_____

📖 Ready, Set, READ!

Read the passage. Then answer the questions.

Didjeridu

The didjeridu may be the world's oldest wind instrument. It is mainly a hollow wooden tube. It is played by blowing into it while buzzing the lips. The "didj" is also called a wooden trumpet, drone pipe, or yidaki. The first didj was made by the Aborigines of northern Australia. They used it during ceremonies.

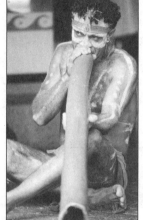

A traditional didj was made of a eucalyptus sapling or branch. Termites naturally eat out the inside of the tree over the course of about a year. Didj makers harvest the wood when they find one of just the right thickness. They cut it to any length they choose, based on the sound they want. Shorter lengths play higher tones; longer lengths player lower tones.

Didj makers usually strip away the outer bark and clean out all the termites. Some smooth or carve the outside. Many use wax to form a soft mouthpiece that has an airtight seal. The didj may be painted or left natural.

1. What kind of instrument is the didjeridu?

   ○ A. rhythm   ○ B. wind   ○ C. string   ○ D. brass

2. Explain how the length of a didj affects its sound. _____

_____

🌀 BrainTeaser 🌀

Go on a word hunt—from your seat! Write an item that includes each word part listed below. Look in your desk, around the room, and out the window for ideas. Words can be any length.

Word part	Item
1. ain	
2. atch	
3. eed	
4. ase	
5. ime	

Word part	Item
6. ish	
7. old	
8. ox	
9. ound	
10. one	

Morning Jumpstarts: Reading, Grade 4 © 2013 Scholastic Teaching Resources

Name _____ Date _____

WORD of the Day

Use the word below in a sentence about someone who has learned much by studying a subject.

scholar: (adj.) *person whose work is to do serious learning or research; expert in a field of study*

_____

_____

Sentence Mender

Rewrite the sentence to make it correct.

They should'nt play there music so lowd when kid's are trying to sleep?

_____

Cursive Quote

Copy the quotation in cursive writing.

Not all readers are leaders, but all leaders are readers.

—Harry S. Truman

_____

_____

_____

Why does Truman advise leaders to read? Write your answer in cursive on another sheet of paper.

Analogy of the Day

Complete the analogy.

Tornado is to **damage** as _____ is to **fever**.

○ A. illness   ○ B. health   ○ C. hurricane   ○ D. fracture

Explain how the analogy works: _____

_____

📖 Ready, Set, READ!

Read the passage. Then answer the questions.

A Mystery of Speed

    Jack "Rabbit" Jones is a swift runner—as fast as lightning. As fast as an arrow. He can get to a pork chop faster than a dog can. He can keep up with a race car. When he plays baseball, he can pop the ball into the air and round the bases before the ball comes down. I know because I saw him do it.

    But recently I heard a story about Rabbit that even I couldn't believe. Nina "The Nose" Ramirez saw it with her own eyes. She told me that she watched Rabbit enter his room, flick off the light switch by the door, and get into his bed before the room was dark.

    Now I know Nina—she's accepts only the facts. And facts are only facts if she sees them with her own two peepers. What Rabbit did sounds impossible, even for him. How did he do it? I need to get back to Nina.

1. What are *peepers*?

    ○ A. spies   ○ B. eyes   ○ C. reporters   ○ D. binoculars

2. Believe it or not, Rabbit did just what Nina saw him do. How do you think he did it?

    Explain. _____

    _____

☺ BrainTeaser ☺

It's a festive summer street fair! What might you see? Write 26 different nouns. Use each letter from *a* to *z* to begin each word. The sentence is started for you.

At the street fair, I saw **a**rtists, **b**ands, **c**lowns, **d**_____

_____

_____

_____

_____

Name _____ Date _____

WORD of the Day

Use the word below in a sentence about taking a relaxing day off.

carefree: (adj.) *without care or worries; happy; cheerful*

_____

_____

Sentence Mender

Rewrite the sentence to make it correct.

Stephen foster the grate American songwriter was born on july 4 1828.

_____

Cursive Quote

Copy the quotation in cursive writing.

No one is perfect. That's why pencils have erasers.

—Anonymous

_____

_____

_____

How can this saying cheer people up? Respond in cursive on another sheet of paper.

Analogy of the Day

Complete the analogy.

Teapot is to **brew** as _____ is to **bake**.

○ A. cake   ○ B. oven   ○ C. coffee   ○ D. turkey

Explain how the analogy works: _____

_____

📖 Ready, Set, READ!

Read the passage. Then answer the questions.

"No Water, No Life"

Sylvia Earle is an ocean scientist, explorer, and teacher. She has spent over 7,000 hours under the sea. She set a record for the deepest solo dive. No wonder her friends call her "Your Deepness!"

Dr. Earle urges everyone to protect our oceans. She hopes her words will convince you because, as she says, "No blue, no green."

- *With every drop of water you drink, every breath you take, you're connected to the sea, no matter where on earth you live.*

- *People ask: Why should I care about the ocean? Because the ocean is the cornerstone of earth's life-support system. It shapes climate and weather. It holds most of life on earth. The ocean holds 97% of earth's water. It's the blue heart of the planet; we should take care of our heart. It's what makes life possible for us.*

- *I believe we should be taking care of the ocean as if our lives depend on it—because they do.*

1. Why are some words in *italics*?

_____

_____

_____

_____

_____

_____

2. Explain "No blue, no green" in your own words.

_____

_____

_____

_____

_____

_____

_____

๑ BrainTeaser ๑

Imagine an adventure to anywhere at any time—past, present, or future! Write 26 different verbs for actions or feelings you might have. Use each letter from *a* to *z* to begin each word. The sentence is started for you.

On my adventure to _____ I might **a**dmire, **b**lush,

_____

_____

_____

Morning Jumpstarts: Reading, Grade 4 © 2013 Scholastic Teaching Resources

Name _____ Date _____

WORD of the Day

Use the word below in a sentence about eating a big meal.

digest: (v.) *to process food inside the body to change it into a form the body can use*

_____

_____

Sentence Mender

Rewrite the sentence to make it correct.

May please I have you autograf prince william.

_____

Cursive Quote

Copy the quotation in cursive writing.

A journey of a thousand miles begins with one step.

—Lao-tzu

_____

_____

_____

What can make taking a first step so hard? Write your answer in cursive on another sheet of paper.

Analogy of the Day

Complete the analogy.

Weak is to **mighty** as _____ is to **noisy**.

○ A. silent   ○ B. strong   ○ C. loud   ○ D. muscle

Explain how the analogy works: _____

_____

📖 Ready, Set, READ!

Read the poem.
Then answer the questions.

Swift Things Are Beautiful
by Elizabeth Coatsworth

Swift things are beautiful:
Swallows and deer,
And lightning that falls
Bright-veined and clear,
Rivers and meteors,
Wind in the wheat,
The strong-withered horse,
The runner's sure feet.

And slow things are beautiful:
The closing of day,
The pause of the wave
That curves downward to spray,
The ember that crumbles,
The opening flower,
And the ox that moves on
In the quiet of power.

1. What is another word for *ember*?
   - ○ A. jewel   ○ C. flame
   - ○ B. cinder   ○ D. cookie

2. What do the things in verse 1 have in common?

   _____

   _____

   _____

   In verse 2?

   _____

   _____

   _____

3. *Withers* are part of a horse's back. What does "strong-withered" mean?

   _____

   _____

   _____

🌀 BrainTeaser 🌀

The sentence in the box has only seven words.
But every word starts with the *same* letter.

**Write a sentence in which every word begins with *h*.
Make it as long as you can.**

> **C**lever **c**ousin **C**lark **c**heerfully
> **c**leans **c**rusty **c**arpets.

_____

_____

_____

_____

Morning Jumpstarts: Reading, Grade 4 © 2013 Scholastic Teaching Resources

Name _____ Date _____

WORD of the Day

Use the word below in a sentence about an early family member you know about.

ancestor: (n.) *someone who came before you in your family, especially earlier than a grandparent*

_____

_____

Sentence Mender

Rewrite the sentence to make it correct.

Are sumer garden in full blum is as pritty as a pitcher.

_____

Cursive Quote

Copy the quotation in cursive writing.

Reading is to the mind what exercise is to the body.

—Joseph Addison

_____

_____

_____

Do you agree with this statement? Explain your view in cursive on another sheet of paper.

Analogy of the Day

Complete the analogy.

Interesting is to **fascinating** as _____ is to **spotless**.

○ A. dull   ○ B. filthy   ○ C. clean   ○ D. spotted

Explain how the analogy works: _____

_____

📖 Ready, Set, READ!

Read the passage. Then answer the questions.

Travel Essay: Following the Astronauts

I can't go to the moon, so I found a closer stand-in. It is Craters of the Moon National Monument in Idaho. The area was formed by volcanic activity hundreds of centuries ago. Burning lava destroyed its plants and animals. However, it left behind new landforms. Many exist nowhere else in the United States. Best of all, it looks like the moon.

I'm a travel writer, not a scientist. But Craters of the Moon really sparked my interest. I wanted to know why it was once a classroom for astronauts! Those pioneers were pilots, not rock experts. NASA scientists wanted them to learn about the rocks so they could know what to look for on the moon.

So the astronauts studied lava flows, rocks, and land features at Craters of the Moon. I did, too. Soon I began to spot differences among the many lava rocks. Park rangers challenged us to see things many visitors miss. I loved my whole trip. And I traveled by van, not by rocket!

1. Astronauts went to Craters of the Moon to
   - O A. travel by van
   - O B. study lava rocks
   - O C. increase strength
   - O D. relax before a flight

2. Which phrase best describes this national monument?
   - O A. Lunar-like landscape
   - O B. Family fun spot
   - O C. Rock heaven
   - O D. Science lab

෨ BrainTeaser ෨

Climb the word ladder to change *corn* to *husk*. Change only one letter at a time. Write the new word on each step.

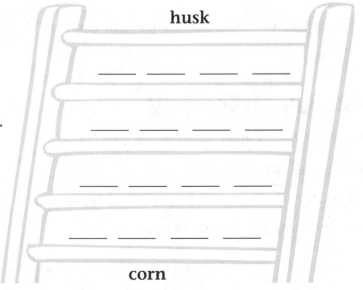

husk

_ _ _ _

_ _ _ _

_ _ _ _

_ _ _ _

corn

Morning Jumpstarts: Reading, Grade 4 © 2013 Scholastic Teaching Resources

Name _____ Date _____

WORD of the Day

Use the word below in a sentence about someone who is easy to trick.

gullible: (adj.) *too ready to believe what people say; easily cheated or tricked*

_____

_____

Sentence Mender

Rewrite the sentence to make it correct.

Lets put some beens cucumbers cheese beats in the salad.

_____

Cursive Quote

Copy the quotation in cursive writing.

Stories are like children. They grow in their own way.

—Madeleine L'Engel

_____

_____

_____

_____

Do you agree with L'Engel that stories are like children? Explain in cursive on another sheet of paper.

Analogy of the Day

Complete the analogy.

Roof is to **house** as _____ is to **room**.

○ A. cabin   ○ B. ceiling   ○ C. kitchen   ○ D. chimney

Explain how the analogy works: _____

_____

📖 Ready, Set, READ!

Read the tall tale. Then answer the questions.

Pecos Bill Rides a Tornado

Everybody in Kansas knew that Pecos Bill could ride anything that moved. No bull or bronco could throw him. Far's I know, Bill never even got thrown when he came here to ride a tornado.

Now Bill wouldn't ride just any tornado! He waited for the wildest twister Kansas ever had. It turned the sky green and black, and roared so loud it woke up half of China. Bill roped that tornado, wrestled it to the ground, and jumped upon its back. The tornado whipped and whirled and spun all the way to Texas. It tied rivers into knots and flattened forests as it went. Bill just hung on, whooping and hooting and sometimes jabbing it with his spurs.

That tornado was beat. So it headed to California to rain itself dry. It let go of so much water on the way that it carved out the Grand Canyon. It was down to near nothing when Bill got off to grab a nap. The tornado hit the ground so hard it sank below sea level. Folks call that spot Death Valley.

1. List three facts hidden in this tall tale.

   1) _____
   _____
   _____

   2) _____
   _____
   _____

   3) _____
   _____
   _____

2. Which real sport has bulls and broncos?
   ○ A. car racing
   ○ B. horse racing
   ○ C. hockey
   ○ D. rodeo

✪ BrainTeaser ✪

What does each saying mean? Read the definitions on the right.
Write the number on the line.

1. I **kept my chin up**.   _____ harder than one can manage

2. Let's not **split hairs**.   _____ what you'd normally expect

3. I'm **in over my head**.   _____ shows no shock or surprise

4. What an **eager beaver**!   _____ argue every little detail

5. She **threw in the towel**.   _____ didn't lose hope

6. He didn't **bat an eyelash**.   _____ hard worker

7. That's **par for the course**.   _____ gave up

Morning Jumpstarts: Reading, Grade 4 © 2013 Scholastic Teaching Resources

Name _____ Date _____

WORD of the Day

Use the word below in a sentence about how to get new members for a club or team.

recruit: (v.) *to get people to join or become new members*

_____

_____

Sentence Mender

Rewrite the sentence to make it correct.

Who winter cote have lost it's hood.

_____

Cursive Quote

Copy the quotation in cursive writing.

A single arrow is easily broken, but not ten in a bundle.

—Japanese proverb

- -

- -

Does this proverb make sense to you? Why? Write your explanation in cursive on another sheet of paper.

Analogy of the Day

Complete the analogy.

Yolk is to **egg** as _____ is to **recipe**.

○ A. shell   ○ B. cook   ○ C. ingredient   ○ D. eat

Explain how the analogy works: _____

_____

📖 Ready, Set, READ!

Read the passage. Then answer the questions.

Heavenly Hats

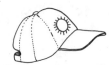

Anthony Leanna got a big idea when he was ten years old. He was visiting his sick grandmother in the hospital. There he saw people who had lost all their hair. It had fallen out because of disease and the medicine they took to help them get well. "I knew that if I was in the hospital and had lost my hair, I would want a hat to wear," he said.

So Anthony started a project. He called it Heavenly Hats. He collected hats to give to patients who needed them. Why did he do this? He says that he wanted to help "people who were going through a very tough time."

Heavenly Hats began in 2001. Since then it has given away over a million hats! You can learn more about Anthony and his project online.

1. How can a hat cheer someone up? _____

_____

2. How does the writer of this piece help you understand Anthony's ideas?

_____

_____

🌀 BrainTeaser 🌀

What do sea monsters eat?

Solve each clue. Then copy each letter into its numbered box to find the answer to the riddle.

• Discovers or locates

 ___ ___ ___ ___ ___
 1   10   6   7   8

• Belt made of ribbon

 ___ ___ ___ ___
 12   5   3   9

• Part between waist and thigh ___ ___ ___
 4   2   11

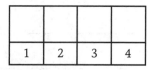

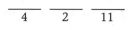
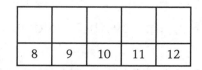

Morning Jumpstarts: Reading, Grade 4 © 2013 Scholastic Teaching Resources

Name _____ Date _____

WORD of the Day

Use the word below in a sentence about a smart safety plan.

policy: (n.) *a plan, rule, or way of acting; program*

_____

_____

Sentence Mender

Rewrite the sentence to make it correct.

Witch one of these knew song did you liked the less?

_____

Cursive Quote

Copy the quotation in cursive writing.

Always laugh when you can. It is cheap medicine.

—Lord Byron

_____

_____

_____

_____

Do you agree with Byron's advice? Write your answer in cursive on another sheet of paper.

Analogy of the Day

Complete the analogy.

Hiker is to **hiking** as _____ is to **entertaining**.

○ A. walking   ○ B. laughing   ○ C. mountain   ○ D. clown

Explain how the analogy works: _____

_____

📖 Ready, Set, READ!

Read the journal entry.
Then answer the questions.

4 June, 1498

We've now been four weeks on the rolling sea. Life aboard the *Mathew* is demanding. It's my first voyage as a ship's boy. I sleep below deck wrapped in part of an old sail. Colin sleeps beside me, but we don't have bunks. It's uncomfortable, and so cramped that we can't stand up straight.

I am but eleven years old, yet my job is better than Colin's. He's a swabber who mops all day to clean the decks. I flip the ship's half-hour glass. It's our only timepiece, so I've been most diligent at my job. Still, we avoid Mr. Stone, the cruel bosun. He's a short-tempered fellow, always ready to snap his cat-o'-nine-tails hard across our tender young hides.

When free, I keep mainly to myself. At times, a friendly seaman will teach me to tie knots, or to splice, wind, and tie the deck ropes. I must learn as much as I can if I hope to become a captain's servant on my next voyage.

1. What is a cat-o'-nine-tails?
   - ○ A. a pet
   - ○ B. a sail
   - ○ C. a whip
   - ○ D. an oar

2. Why would the boy hope to become a captain's servant?

   _____

   _____

   _____

   _____

   _____

   _____

   _____

   _____

🌀 BrainTeaser 🌀

How many different words can you spell with letters from the word *denominators*?
Every word must have at least three letters. List them here.

_____

_____

_____

_____

Morning Jumpstarts: Reading, Grade 4 © 2013 Scholastic Teaching Resources

Name _____ Date _____

ᐁᐊᐁᐊᐁᐊᐁᐊᐁᐊᐁᐊᐁᐊᐁ
WORD
of the Day
ᐁᐊᐁᐊᐁᐊᐁᐊᐁᐊᐁᐊᐁᐊᐁ

Use the word below in a sentence about a rude remark.

flippant: (adj.) *lacking respect or seriousness; rude; jokey*

_____

_____

Sentence Mender

Rewrite the sentence to make it correct.

Its total impossable to keep your eyes open when you sneezed

_____

Cursive Quote

Copy the quotation in cursive writing.

No act of kindness, no matter how small, is ever wasted.

—Aesop

_____

_____

_____

How can a small kind act make a lasting impression? Write your answer in cursive on another sheet of paper.

Analogy of the Day

Complete the analogy.

Glass is to **shattered** as _____ is to **torn**.

○ A. cry   ○ B. brick   ○ C. paper   ○ D. window

Explain how the analogy works: _____

_____

Side B

📖 Ready, Set, READ!

Read the passage. Then answer the questions.

Burying the Hatchet

Have you ever heard the expression "Let's bury the hatchet?" A hatchet is an axe. The expression refers to an old custom that some Native American groups used to end war and make peace.

Chiefs decided when to stop fighting. They held a ceremony together. Each offered to bury his own hatchet to "seal the deal." They might pick a spot beneath a tree or in a riverbed. This gesture was an act of trust, like shaking hands. It showed that both chiefs were willing to put aside their differences and move on.

The expression "to bury the hatchet" means to forget about disagreements and be friends again. Suppose two brothers who want a pet aren't getting along. They might agree to "bury the hatchet" to make a point to their parents. It would show that they are finally ready to cooperate for the pet.

1. Why would both chiefs give their hatchets for the peace ceremony?

_____

_____

2. How does the author explain the meaning of this expression?

_____

_____

🌀 BrainTeaser 🌀

Solve the puzzle.

It has a two-letter word on top and an eight-letter word at the bottom. Going down, each word uses the same letters as the word above it, plus one more, and then rearranged.

Clues:
- On, by, or near
- Had food
- Group of soccer players
- Tried to explain
- Related to the mind
- Shelves over a fireplace
- Medical problems

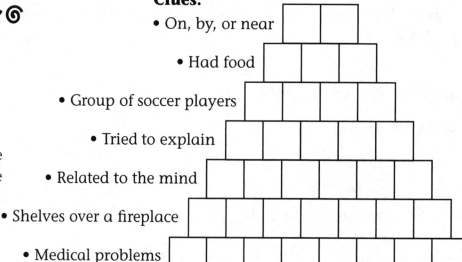

84

Morning Jumpstarts: Reading, Grade 4 © 2013 Scholastic Teaching Resources

Name _____ Date _____

WORD of the Day

Use the word below in a sentence to tell what "raised eyebrows" might mean.

indicate: (v.) *to show, prove, or point out clearly; specify*

_____

_____

Sentence Mender

Rewrite the sentence to make it correct.

A ostriches eye is bigger then it's brain!

_____

Cursive Quote

Copy the quotation in cursive writing.

Any kid will run any errand for you if you ask at bedtime.

—Red Skelton

_____

_____

_____

Do you think that Skelton is correct? Explain your views in cursive on another sheet of paper.

Analogy of the Day

Complete the analogy.

Relax is to **tighten** as _____ is to **fail**.

○ A. loose   ○ B. rest   ○ C. flunk   ○ D. pass

Explain how the analogy works: _____

_____

📖 Ready, Set, READ!

Read the myth. Then answer the questions.

Jaguar, Master of Fire   A *Myth From South America*

In ancient days, humans of the jungle were weak creatures. They had no weapons. Finding enough food to eat was a daily struggle. If they caught an animal, they had to eat it raw because they did not yet have fire.

Jaguar was stronger and wiser. This sleek cat had powerful legs, keen ears and eyes, and sharp teeth. His bows and arrows made him an expert hunter. Jaguar, Master of Fire, cooked his meat.

Jaguar was kind then. He pitied the humans. One day Jaguar came upon a starving man. He gently led the weak man to his den. Jaguar showed him fire. Jaguar grilled meat to feed the man, who ate with ravenous pleasure. Jaguar showed his weapons and taught the man to hunt with them.

The man owed his life to Jaguar. But he realized that Jaguar had given him new power. Alas, the man repaid Jaguar's kindness with cruelty. He killed Jaguar's wife and stole his fire. Since then, humans and jaguars have feared each other. Humans know that jaguars wait to take revenge on them.

1. What made Jaguar stronger and wiser than ancient humans? _____

_____

2. How did Jaguar's encounter with the man change both of them? _____

_____

☙ BrainTeaser ❧

The word bank lists astronomy words.
Each word is hidden in the puzzle.
Find and circle each word.

Word Bank

ASTEROID	GALAXY	PLANET
COMET	METEOR	SATELLITE
CORONA	MILKY WAY	SOLAR
ECLIPSE	NEBULA	SOLSTICE
EQUINOX	ORBIT	STAR
FLARES	PHASE	SUNSPOTS

```
E M G C E W B K R O E T E M
C I S E O S I F G A L A X Y
I L V O L M A Z P C T S O B
T K S S Q E E H V H W S Y R
S Y U S L T K T P Z Z T S B
L W N D W I D I O R E T S A
O A S M G L J I B N O E X S
S Y P N S L L B A R C O E C
L H O E O E H L B L N R Y O
I K T B L T P I I I A X W R
X A S U A A T P U L A H X O
X V P L R S S Q F L O B X N
A T S A M E E B A L B D I A
```

Morning Jumpstarts: Reading, Grade 4 © 2013 Scholastic Teaching Resources

Name _____ Date _____

WORD of the Day

Use the word below in a sentence about a school volunteer.

volunteer: (n.) *a person who works without pay; someone who offers help, advice, or service by choice*

_____

_____

Sentence Mender

Rewrite the sentence to make it correct.

The worlds heavyest onion wayed more than a mans head!

_____

Cursive Quote

Copy the quotation in cursive writing.

We can learn something new any time we believe we can.

—Virginia Satir

How can believing lead to success? Write your answer in cursive on another sheet of paper.

Analogy of the Day

Complete the analogy.

Nickel is to **coin** as _____ is to **tool.**

○ A. wrench   ○ B. dime   ○ C. bill   ○ D. plumber

Explain how the analogy works: _____

_____

📖 Ready, Set, READ!

Read the book review. Then answer the questions.

A Review of *Peter and the Starcatchers*

Peter and the Starcatchers is a novel by Dave Barry and Ridley Pearson. It explains how Peter Pan came to be. It's a long book, but I loved it. I even let my parents borrow it!

This book has many parts that would be familiar to readers who know the original Peter Pan story. You meet orphans, pirates, mermaids, and a crocodile. There is a shipwreck, some stardust, many secrets, and dashing swordfights. Black Stache is the pirate who later becomes Captain Hook. The authors made up some new characters, too, such as Molly. She tries to keep the stardust away from the pirates. She also helps Peter become the character originally created over a century ago.

This book switches moods a lot. It is wild, silly, playful, scary, and sad. What I liked best is that it mixed goofy humor with old-fashioned story-telling. I bet it would make a great read-aloud—if you have lots of time!

1. A sequel is a later installment of a story. This book is a *prequel*. How would you explain what a prequel is? _____

   _____

2. The reviewer liked the many mood switches in this book. How can mood switches keep a reader interested? _____

   _____

⊚ BrainTeaser ⊚

Each sentence below has two blanks. Both use the same letters to form different three-letter words. Fill them in.

1. Only two of the _____ boys can reach the top of the _____.

2. Use this soothing _____ for the cut on your _____.

3. There is a bear's _____ at the _____ of that path.

4. Soldiers in _____ may have to eat _____ food.

5. Is it okay for _____ to _____ your phone?

6. _____ that you _____ the bike, you can paint it pink.

88

Name _____ Date _____

WORD of the Day

Use the word below in a sentence about a foolish choice.

misguided: (adj.) *led to make mistakes or do wrong; foolish*

_____

_____

Sentence Mender

Rewrite the sentence to make it correct.

Each tiger have unique strips almost like people has fingerprince.

_____

Cursive Quote

Copy the quotation in cursive writing.

It's nice to be important, but it's more important to be nice.

—Author unknown

....

....

....

Explain what this saying means to you. Write your answer in cursive on another sheet of paper.

Analogy of the Day

Complete the analogy.

Spatula is to **cook** as _____ is to **archer**.

○ A. knife   ○ B. bow   ○ C. athlete   ○ D. medal

Explain how the analogy works: _____

_____

📖 Ready, Set, READ!

Read the passage. Then answer the questions.

Henna Body Art

Mehndi (MEN-dee) is the ancient art of body painting. It has been used in India and the Middle East for centuries. Mehndi designs look like tattoos, but they aren't. Designs are painted onto the skin.

First the artist prepares Mehndi "ink." This is done by crushing the leaves of the henna plant. The artist grinds them into powder, and then mixes in oils and other liquids to form a dark green paste.

Then the artist uses brushes or squeeze tubes to draw the design right onto the skin. It takes hours for large or detailed designs. After the design is done, the artist coats it with sugary lemon juice. This helps the design dry without smudging.

The next day, the wearer scrapes the paste off. By now, the henna has stained the skin and has turned from dark green to red-orange. By the day after, the mehndi turns brown. It can stay on for two or three weeks.

1. How would you describe the structure of the passage about mehndi?
   - ○ A. cause/effect
   - ○ B. question/answer
   - ○ C. time order
   - ○ D. problem/solution

2. How are mehndi and tattoos alike? _____
   _____
   _____
   _____

   How are they different?
   _____
   _____
   _____
   _____

🌀 BrainTeaser 🌀

Use the clues to complete each word that includes *j*.

1. Slightly open, like a door   ___ j ___ ___

2. An American form of music   j ___ ___ ___

3. Pop out of the DVD player   ___ j ___ ___ ___

4. Opposite of minor   ___ ___ j ___ ___

5. Stringed instrument   ___ ___ ___ j ___

6. Take pleasure in   ___ ___ j ___ ___

7. Thing or item   ___ ___ j ___ ___ ___

90

Morning Jumpstarts: Reading, Grade 4 © 2013 Scholastic Teaching Resources

Name _____ Date _____

WORD of the Day

Use the word below in a sentence about why you might rest your feet on a stool or pillow.

elevate: (v.) *to raise or lift up*

_____

_____

Sentence Mender

Rewrite the sentence to make it correct.

Yesterday she was two sick to go to school but today he be better.

_____

Cursive Quote

Copy the quotation in cursive writing.

Never look down on anybody unless you're helping him up.

—Jesse Jackson

_____

_____

_____

What does Jackson mean to "look down on" someone? Write your answer in cursive on another sheet of paper.

Analogy of the Day

Complete the analogy.

Trunk is to **elephant** as _____ is to **fish**.

○ A. hook   ○ B. ocean   ○ C. gill   ○ D. tank

Explain how the analogy works: _____

_____

📖 Ready, Set, READ!

Read the passage. Then answer the questions.

The Hindu New Year

People everywhere mark special events with candles, lamps, or other lights. Diwali is the Hindu New Year. The word *Diwali* means "row of lamps." People light the Diwali lamps to welcome Lord Rama. They honor his victory over evil spirits. The lamps also help Lakshmi, the goddess of wealth, to find each home.

Diwali comes each fall. It lasts for three to five days, depending on local customs. *Diya* are small lamps used at Diwali. They are small bowls that hold oil. A cotton wick burns in the oil. People set diya all around their homes.

These are typical plans for the five days of Diwali.

- Day 1: Families get excited and ready. They clean, shop, and cook.
- Day 2: The diya are lit. Fireworks keep away evil spirits.
- Day 3: This is the main day of Diwali. There are many festive events.
- Day 4: This is the time for feasting and fun!
- Day 5: On this day, brothers and sisters honor their family bonds.

1. At what time of year do people celebrate Diwali?

   ○ A. winter   ○ B. spring   ○ C. summer   ○ D. autumn

2. What is the purpose of the list? _____

   _____

๑ BrainTeaser ๑

Write the name of your favorite celebrity. Write 26 different adjectives to describe that person. Use each letter from *a* to *z* to begin each word. The sentence is started for you.

My favorite celebrity is _____ because he or she is

_____

_____

_____

_____

_____

Morning Jumpstarts: Reading, Grade 4 © 2013 Scholastic Teaching Resources

Name _____ Date _____

WORD of the Day

Use the word below in a sentence about a smart study plan.

strategy: (n.) *clever plan or system; skillful approach*

_____

_____

Sentence Mender

Rewrite the sentence to make it correct.

Yes jared prattice his piano lessin for fivteen minits a day

_____

Cursive Quote

Copy the quotation in cursive writing.

When you're thirsty it's too late to think about digging a well.

—Japanese proverb

_____

_____

_____

What is another way to express this same idea? Write your answer in cursive on another sheet of paper.

Analogy of the Day

Complete the analogy.

Honey is to **sticky** as _____ is to **warm**.

○ A. ice   ○ B. soup   ○ C. freezer   ○ D. river

Explain how the analogy works: _____

_____

Side B

📖 Ready, Set, READ!

Read the story. Then answer the questions.

Mysti hadn't slept well. A series of crazy dreams kept her tossing and turning all night. By 4:45 A.M., she gave up and decided to read. She reached out to switch on her bedside lamp but recoiled in shock. She opened her mouth to scream, but no sound came out. Something was terribly wrong.

Mysti's long arms were now stumpy and scaly. She saw three long claws where her fingers should have been. Her eyesight, usually so sharp, was blurry. She headed to the mirror. But instead of walking across the room, Mysti found herself scuttling along on all fours, low to the ground. A bony tail trailed behind her.

Mysti had turned into an armadillo! Her tank-like body was covered with jointed, armor-like plates that made it hard to move. She desperately hoped that she was still dreaming. If not, this was going to be a difficult day . . .

1. What was Mysti's first clue that something was very wrong?
   - O A. She had a tail.
   - O B. She had bad dreams.
   - O C. Her vision was weak.
   - O D. She had scales and claws.

2. Another word that means the same as *scuttling* is
   - O A. hopping
   - O B. limping
   - O C. scampering
   - O D. slithering

๑ BrainTeaser ๑

What does each saying mean? Read the definitions on the right.
Write the number on the line.

1. I'm **in hot water** now.

2. They are **going bananas!**

3. He's the **apple of my eye**.

4. You **have a heart of gold**.

5. **Look for the silver lining**.

6. It's time to **crack the books!**

7. That's **how the cookie crumbles**.

_____ Good can come even from bad.

_____ What else would you expect?

_____ acting emotional, wild, crazy

_____ the one I love most dearly

_____ are kind, caring, honest

_____ expecting big trouble

_____ study hard

Morning Jumpstarts: Reading, Grade 4 © 2013 Scholastic Teaching Resources

Name _____ Date _____

WORD of the Day

Use the word below in a sentence about learning a new dance.

awkward: (adj.) *clumsy; without grace or skill; embarrassing*

_____

_____

Sentence Mender

Rewrite the sentence to make it correct.

She's truely faverit athalete is socker player david beckham.

_____

Cursive Quote

Copy the quotation in cursive writing.

Don't let what you can't do stop you from what you can do.

—John Wooden

- - - - - - - - - - - - - - - -

- - - - - - - - - - - - - - - -

John Wooden was a great basketball coach. How might his statement inspire people on or off the basketball court? Write your answer in cursive on another sheet of paper.

Analogy of the Day

Complete the analogy.

Find is to **discover** as _____ is to **watch**.

○ A. wrist ○ B. avoid ○ C. lose ○ D. view

Explain how the analogy works: _____

_____

📖 Ready, Set, READ!

Read the passage. Then answer the questions.

Health is the state of being well. Most people think health just means not being sick. This is true, but it's not the full story. Picture a triangle with three equal sides to see health in a new way.

Each side of the triangle stands for a different part of health: physical, mental, and social. People who care for all three parts can gain in overall strength, balance, and happiness.

• **Physical** health is about how the body works. It involves the foods you choose, the exercise you get, rest, sleep, and hygiene (keeping clean). This is the kind of health most people think of first.

• **Mental** health is about how the mind works, thinks, and feels. It involves ideas, emotions, and reactions, all of which affect your views on life.

• **Social** health is about getting along with people— family, friends, and others. It is about care, respect, and support—both giving and getting.

1. How does the triangle figure help explain this idea?

_____

_____

2. Which term best relates to social health?
   ○ A. hygiene   ○ B. emotions   ○ C. cooperation   ○ D. fitness

☯ BrainTeaser ☯

Find the extra word in each sentence and cross it out.

1. Some people are able to speak three or languages.

2. A mule is a cross word between a horse and a donkey.

3. The sign warns hikers to watch tower out for rattlesnakes.

4. I always sit in a window seat belt if there is one available.

5. The Lowry Park Zoo is a very popular with family visitors.

6. The class will put on a play about lumberjack Paul Bunyan and.

Morning Jumpstarts: Reading, Grade 4 © 2013 Scholastic Teaching Resources

Name _____ Date _____

Morning Jumpstarts: Reading, Grade 4 © 2013 Scholastic Teaching Resources

WORD of the Day

Use the word below in a sentence about using a hand lens.

magnify: (v.) *to make something look larger than it really is*

_____

_____

Sentence Mender

Rewrite the sentence to make it correct.

Pleas leaf your sootcase hear why'll you by you're ticket.

_____

Cursive Quote

Copy the quotation in cursive writing.

Be careful what you say because it can hurt more than a knife.

—Indonesian proverb

_____

_____

_____

How can words hurt as much as a knife wound can? Write your answer in cursive on another sheet of paper.

Analogy of the Day

Complete the analogy.

Leg is to **limb** as _____ is to **music**.

O A. flute   O B. arm   O C. drama   O D. jazz

Explain how the analogy works: _____

_____

📖 Ready, Set, READ!

Read the story. Then answer the questions.

Inside a Square Foot

Henry's task was to write an observer's journal. The teacher gave the assignment. Henry guessed he'd finish in a flash until she added, "Good observers take their time. They look slowly and carefully, close and hard. Give yourself time to get acquainted with the space inside your frame. You can't see everything in one glance."

The class trudged out to the hillside. Henry chose a shady spot and sat on his knees. He set his empty frame on the grass and started scanning the square inside it. At first, he saw only a solid green patch. Then he stooped down extremely close.

That's when his square foot revealed texture and life. Blades of grass stood at every height and angle. They were yellow, brown, and a dozen shades of green. Ants marched through as if on a mission. Henry noticed twigs, a rusty nail, and a striped feather. A ladybug crawled onto the feather, adding a splash of bright color. Henry grabbed his clipboard and pencil . . .

1. What did Henry think of the assignment at first? _____

_____

2. How did his attitude change? _____

_____

🌀 BrainTeaser 🌀

Use the clues to complete each word that includes *cap*.

1. Flowing garment   C A P ___ ___

2. Summary   ___ ___ C A P

3. Adventure   C A P ___ ___

4. Get away   ___ ___ C A P ___

5. Cover for a car's wheel ___ ___ ___ C A P

6. Words below a picture   C A P ___ ___ ___ ___

7. City where government is C A P ___ ___ ___ ___

8. Ship commander   C A P ___ ___ ___ ___

98

JUMPSTART 46

Name _____ Date _____

WORD of the Day

Use the word below in a sentence about a sports stadium.

capacity: (n.) *the amount of space inside; volume; the greatest measure an object can hold*

_____

_____

Sentence Mender

Rewrite the sentence to make it correct.

We finish two hole water melons at the class picknick.

_____

Cursive Quote

Copy the quotation in cursive writing.

It's not what happens to you, but how you react to it that matters.
                                                                    —Epictetus

_____

_____

_____

This saying is about 2,000 years old. Do you think it is true today?
Write your answer in cursive on another sheet of paper.

Analogy of the Day

Complete the analogy.

State is to **nation** as _____ is to **band**.

○ A. drummer   ○ B. capital   ○ C. song   ○ D. Virginia

Explain how the analogy works: _____

_____

Morning Jumpstarts: Reading, Grade 4 © 2013 Scholastic Teaching Resources

99

📖 Ready, Set, READ!

Read the passage. Then answer the questions.

Supply and Demand

Economics is the science of buying and selling. It looks at how money affects us. Two big economic ideas are supply and demand.

Supply is how much of something is available. If you have 8 muffins to sell, your supply is 8. *Demand* is how much of something people want. If 10 people want muffins, the demand is 10. Supply and demand are related. They are usually discussed together. Prices can help explain the connection.

If the demand is high, the price usually goes up. If the demand goes down, the price usually goes down. Take sneakers. Popular new sneakers can cost a lot. This is because the demand for them is high. Older sneakers are usually a lot cheaper. This is because fewer people want them. When the demand is down, so is the price.

1. What is economics?
   ○ A. supply and demand
   ○ B. study of buying and selling
   ○ C. study of shopping
   ○ D. science of selling sneakers

2. What might cause prices to rise?
   ○ A. decrease in interest
   ○ B. increase in shopping malls
   ○ C. decrease in demand
   ○ D. increase in demand

๑ BrainTeaser ๑

Write the missing word for each three-word expression.

1. flesh and _____

2. knock on _____

3. bite your _____

4. rule of _____

5. rise and _____

6. _____ of cake

7. _____ and then

8. _____ the bucket

9. _____ from scratch

10. _____ your horses

Morning Jumpstarts: Reading, Grade 4 © 2013 Scholastic Teaching Resources

JUMPSTART 47

Name _____ Date _____

WORD of the Day

Use the word below in a sentence about a roaring noise.

deafening: (adj.) *stunningly loud; earsplitting; booming*

_____

_____

Sentence Mender

Rewrite the sentence to make it correct.

Lake huron is the forth deepist of the five Great lake's.

_____

Cursive Quote

Copy the quotation in cursive writing.

I hear and I forget. I see and I remember. I do and I understand.
—Chinese proverb

Pretend you are the "I" in this proverb. Does it fit you? Write your answer in cursive on another sheet of paper.

Analogy of the Day

Complete the analogy.

Lens is to **camera** as _____ is to **computer**.

○ A. film   ○ B. desk   ○ C. monitor   ○ D. library

Explain how the analogy works: _____

_____

JUMPSTART 47

📖 Ready, Set, READ!

Read the passage. Then answer the questions.

An Enchanting Imp

The impish Puck has caused trouble for centuries. In older times, people believed in fairies and spirits, both good and evil. It was easy to blame them when things were confusing or went wrong.

William Shakespeare made Puck the key trouble-maker in his comedy *A Midsummer Night's Dream*. "I am that merry wanderer of the night," Puck says. He's a charming but annoying spirit. He plays tricks for fun. He makes fools of the humans to amuse the fairies.

This 500-year-old play is like a goofy sit-com. It takes place at night in an enchanted forest. Puck causes a string of mishaps and mix-ups. He makes a love potion but gives it to the wrong people! Actors rehearse a play to put on at a wedding. Puck finds their acting so bad that he turns one of them into a donkey! This makes their play even worse!

But in a comedy, things get sorted out by the end. Puck untangles all the messes, and everyone lives happily ever after.

1. Why were people long ago so willing to believe in fairies and spirits?

_____

2. Which is the opposite of *comedy*?
- ○ A. humor
- ○ B. fiction
- ○ C. tragedy
- ○ D. poetry

🌀 BrainTeaser 🌀

How long a word link can you make? Link words by starting a new word with the *last* letter of the word before. This word link uses colors:

yellow → white → eggshell → lavender

Continue the link of American places started below.
Think of towns, cities, islands, lakes, rivers, national parks, or states.

Idaho → Oklahoma → Albany → _____

_____

_____

_____

Morning Jumpstarts: Reading, Grade 4 © 2013 Scholastic Teaching Resources

Name _____ Date _____

WORD of the Day

Use the word below in a sentence about a doctor who is an expert in a certain branch of medicine.

specialize: (v.) *to make a special study of something or follow a certain branch of work*

_____

_____

Sentence Mender

Rewrite the sentence to make it correct.

The, axolotl or mexican walking fish, we now as a salamandar.

_____

Cursive Quote

Copy the quotation in cursive writing.

It does not matter how slow you go so long as you do not stop.

—Confucius

Explain in your own words what Confucius means. Write your answer in cursive on another sheet of paper.

Analogy of the Day

Complete the analogy.

Smart is to **brilliant** as _____ is to **beautiful**.

O A. charming   O B. slow   O C. pretty   O D. sharp

Explain how the analogy works: _____

_____

Ready, Set, READ!

Read the passage. Then answer the questions.

Three Branches of Government

The U.S. Constitution gives the rules of how our country is set up. It says that our government in Washington, D.C., will have three branches, or parts. The branches are equal. But each has a different job. Each branch has a different leader. Each works in a different place. Each branch has ways to affect the other two.

The chart can help explain the jobs.

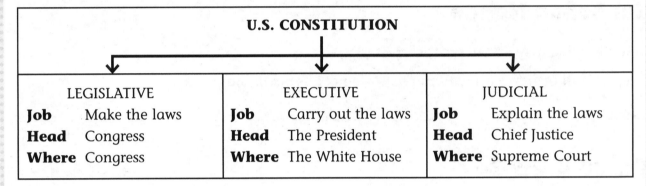

U.S. CONSTITUTION		
LEGISLATIVE	**EXECUTIVE**	**JUDICIAL**
Job Make the laws	**Job** Carry out the laws	**Job** Explain the laws
Head Congress	**Head** The President	**Head** Chief Justice
Where Congress	**Where** The White House	**Where** Supreme Court

1. Where does the Judicial branch work? _____

2. Which branch makes the laws? _____

3. A Constitutional title for the President is the

   ○ A. Chief Justice   ○ B. Chief Executive   ○ C. Head of Congress

⑨ BrainTeaser ⑥

What do lazy dogs do for fun and exercise?

Solve each clue. Then copy each letter into its numbered box to find the answer to the riddle.

• Decode the words   — — — —
                      8 5 13 11

• Small run-down hut — — — — —
                     15 2 7 1 9

• Scuff your knee — — — — — —
                   4 12 14 3 6 10

1	2	3	4	5

6	7	8	9	10	11

12	13	14	15

Name _____ Date _____

WORD of the Day

Use the word below in a sentence about taking something apart to see how it works.

mechanism: (n.) *a system of working parts in a machine*

_____

_____

Sentence Mender

Rewrite the sentence to make it correct.

He like her iced tee with alot of shugar or honie.

_____

Cursive Quote

Copy the quotation in cursive writing.

Patience: You get the chicken by hatching the egg, not by smashing it.

—Arnold H. Glasow

- -

- -

What makes it so hard to be patient? Write your answer in cursive on another sheet of paper.

Analogy of the Day

Complete the analogy.

Steeple is to **church** as _____ is to **cake.**

○ A. sweet   ○ B. candle   ○ C. steep   ○ D. layer

Explain how the analogy works: _____

_____

Morning Jumpstarts: Reading, Grade 4 © 2013 Scholastic Teaching Resources

📖 Ready, Set, READ!

Read the story. Then answer the questions.

I began hiking around the lake one misty October dawn. The bears and mountain lions were out seeking food. Signs posted at the trailhead warned people to hike in groups and not to bring pets along. They also advised making plenty of noise. So I hugged the lake shore and avoided any trail leading away from it into the thicker woods. I whistled as I walked.

I admit it, I was nervous. I kept my eyes peeled for anything moving that wasn't me. I walked for about ten minutes when I saw them: big fresh paw prints. I stopped dead in my tracks and examined them. These were nothing like the tracks house pets make. One big kitty had recently been here!

I was in no mood to startle a mountain lion or bump into a bear. I did an about-face that would suit a general. Then I sprinted to the safety of my car.

1. Why did the narrator whistle? _____

_____

2. What does it mean to "hug" the lake shore? _____

_____

3. Which would make the best title for this passage?
   ○ A. Hiking a Trail   ○ C. A Misty Dawn
   ○ B. Big Kitty   ○ D. A Quick Turn-Around

⦿ BrainTeaser ⦿

Homophones are words that sound the same but have different spellings and meanings.
Write the correct word in each sentence.

1. That belt is too big for his _____.   **waist** *or* **waste**

2. Please _____ out your wet swim suit.   **ring** *or* **wring**

3. We dropped an _____ into the lake.   **ore** *or* **oar**

4. That bad cough left me a little _____.   **hoarse** *or* **horse**

5. Old paints used to be made with _____.   **lead** *or* **led**

6. Adult lions have such thick _____!   **mains** *or* **manes**

7. Today the dentist saw nine _____.   **patience** *or* **patients**

Morning Jumpstarts: Reading, Grade 4 © 2013 Scholastic Teaching Resources

Name _____ Date _____

WORD of the Day

Use the word below in a sentence about a call for help.

urgent: (adj.) *very important; needing serious action now*

_____

_____

Sentence Mender

Rewrite the sentence to make it correct.

Sorry son but You ain't the one who get to deside.

_____

Cursive Quote

Copy the quotation in cursive writing.

Even if happiness forgets you a little bit, never completely forget about it.

—Jacques Prévert

. . . .

. . . .

_____

How do you feel about Prévert's advice? Write your answer in cursive on another sheet of paper.

Analogy of the Day

Complete the analogy.

Thirsty is to **drink** as _____ is to **doze**.

O A. tired   O B. hungry   O C. bed   O D. eat

Explain how the analogy works: _____

_____

Ready, Set, READ!

Read the passage. Then answer the questions.

A Noisy Dish?

"I'll have the bubble and squeak, please."

You don't hear people order that very often, do you? But in Great Britain, people do it all the time. Bubble and squeak is a common dish there. It is a classic comfort food made with leftover vegetables.

The main part of the dish is mashed potato. It is the glue that holds together everything else. The leftover vegetables may be carrots, Brussels sprouts, turnips, rutabagas, cabbage, leeks, spinach, beans, or onions. Bubble and squeak is a tasty way to get kids to eat their veggies. Add meat or fried eggs and you have a hearty lunch.

You might wonder about the dish's odd name. Some foods are named for the way they look, feel, smell, or taste. Examples include black-eyed peas, animal crackers, sloppy joes, or sauerkraut. Bubble and squeak is named for the *sounds* the potatoes make as they cook. First they bubble as they boil. Then they squeak as they fry. Eat up!

1. Where is bubble and squeak a popular dish? _____

_____

2. How did the dish get its name? _____

_____

BrainTeaser

Complete the category chart. The letters above each column
tell the first letter for each word.

	F	E	L	T
Foods				
Nations				
Movies				
Mammals				

Morning Jumpstarts: Reading, Grade 4 © 2013 Scholastic Teaching Resources

Answers

Jumpstart 1
Word of the Day: Check students' sentences for accurate usage of the term.
Sentence Mender: Our three puppies are Mo, Curly, and Larry. Note: the series comma before *and* is optional.
Cursive Quote: Check students' handwriting for accuracy and legibility. Responses will vary.
Analogy of the Day: D; (object-location analogy) Check that students' answers are reasonable.
Ready, Set, Read! 1. The balls of fluff were the two mutts. **2.** Answers will vary; sample answer: I think they decided to adopt both puppies.
Brainteaser: Possible answer: limp, lime, line, fine

Jumpstart 2
Word of the Day: Check students' sentences for accurate usage of the term.
Sentence Mender: Can you name all fifty states of the United States?
Cursive Quote: Check students' handwriting for accuracy and legibility. Responses will vary.
Analogy of the Day: B; (synonyms analogy) Check that students' answers are reasonable.
Ready, Set, Read! 1. They do whatever work is needed on a farm, like picking fruit. **2.** Trey means that the taste is so amazing, his mouth will be delighted.
Brainteaser: 1. shoes **2.** shook **3.** shore **4.** should **5.** shower **6.** shovels

Jumpstart 3
Word of the Day: Check students' sentences for accurate usage of the term.
Sentence Mender: No, I did not eat the last piece of candy.
Cursive Quote: Check students' handwriting for accuracy and legibility. Responses will vary.
Analogy of the Day: C; (cause-and-effect analogy) Check that students' answers are reasonable.
Ready, Set, Read! 1. B **2.** The merchant was ashamed that the child asked a question that was impossible for him to answer.
Brainteaser: 1. high **2.** comic **3.** going **4.** erase **5.** label **6.** razor **7.** dried **8.** yearly **9.** typist

Jumpstart 4
Word of the Day: Check students' sentences for accurate usage of the term.
Sentence Mender: Bruno, who walks my dog, also waters the plants.
Cursive Quote: Check students' handwriting for accuracy and legibility. Responses will vary.
Analogy of the Day: A; (antonyms analogy) Check that students' answers are reasonable.
Ready, Set, Read! 1. The party is to celebrate Dad's new job. **2.** Potluck means that the guests must bring a food (in this case, a dessert) to share and nobody knows what may turn up.
Brainteaser: 1. sore **2.** lost **3.** rage **4.** lift **5.** crate **6.** alter/later **7.** sloop/loops/spool **8.** steer/reset

Jumpstart 5
Word of the Day: Check students' sentences for accurate usage of the term.
Sentence Mender: Tomorrow we will be visiting a bakery.
Cursive Quote: Check students' handwriting for accuracy and legibility. Responses will vary.
Analogy of the Day: D; (class-example analogy) Check that students' answers are reasonable.
Ready, Set, Read! 1. B **2.** Lion saw his own reflection in the pool.
Brainteaser: 1. Don't open your eyes yet. **2.** Would you like a second helping? **3.** Tomorrow is the first day of June. **4.** Could you bring the salad to the table?

Jumpstart 6
Word of the Day: Check students' sentences for accurate usage of the term.
Sentence Mender: I'm reading the book Lizard Music by Daniel Pinkwater.
Cursive Quote: Check students' handwriting for accuracy and legibility. Responses will vary.
Analogy of the Day: B; (antonyms analogy) Check that students' answers are reasonable.
Ready, Set, Read! 1. D **2.** C
Brainteaser: Answers will vary; sample answers: **1.** clank **2.** crackles **3.** swoosh **4.** splat **5.** clatter

Jumpstart 7
Word of the Day: Check students' sentences for accurate usage of the term.
Sentence Mender: Turn up the heat because it is too cold in here.
Cursive Quote: Check students' handwriting for accuracy and legibility. Responses will vary.
Analogy of the Day: B; (part-whole analogy) Check that students' answers are reasonable.
Ready, Set, Read! 1. They have the same number of lines and the same rhyme scheme. They also begin with the same words. **2.** They differ in how Isabella's family members reacted to her caterpillar. **3.** Her great-grandmother liked it the most.
Brainteaser: 1. words **2.** gold **3.** basket **4.** policy **5.** leap **6.** perfect **7.** worm **8.** tricks

Jumpstart 8
Word of the Day: Check students' sentences for accurate usage of the term.
Sentence Mender: The older children can make their own lunches.
Cursive Quote: Check students' handwriting for accuracy and legibility. Responses will vary.
Analogy of the Day: D; (object-location analogy) Check that students' answers are reasonable.
Ready, Set, Read! 1. Meaning 4. **2.** Sample sentence: The lantern sent out a beam of light into the cave.
Brainteaser: 1. bag tag **2.** mouse house **3.** book nook **4.** stamp champ **5.** strange change **6.** worn horn

Jumpstart 9
Word of the Day: Check students' sentences for accurate usage of the term.
Sentence Mender: Jason asked, "Can you help me find my keys?"
Cursive Quote: Check students' handwriting for accuracy and legibility. Responses will vary.
Analogy of the Day: B; (degree of meaning or synonyms analogy) Check that students' answers are reasonable.
Ready, Set, Read! 1. D **2.** Answers will vary; sample answer: Scott wanted to let someone know where he was and why he wouldn't be home that night.
Brainteaser: 1. witty kitty **2.** boulder holder **3.** kitten mitten **4.** stranger danger **5.** jelly belly **6.** lucky ducky

Jumpstart 10
Word of the Day: Check students' sentences for accurate usage of the term.
Sentence Mender: The science teacher gives us short quizzes every day.
Cursive Quote: Check students' handwriting for accuracy and legibility. Responses will vary.
Analogy of the Day: C; (degree of meaning or synonyms analogy) Check that students' answers are reasonable.
Ready, Set, Read! 1. It's hard because the outside points are all different distances from the center. **2.** Answers will vary; sample answer: Those two states are not attached to the other 48.
Brainteaser: (Top to bottom) polka, twist, tango, ballet, bolero, reel; partner

Jumpstart 11
Word of the Day: Check students' sentences for accurate usage of the term.
Sentence Mender: How many legs do spiders have?
Cursive Quote: Check students' handwriting for accuracy and legibility. Responses will vary.
Analogy of the Day: A; (object-action analogy) Check that students' answers are reasonable.
Ready, Set, Read! 1. C **2.** B
Brainteaser: 1. plain **2.** supporter **3.** first **4.** tremble **5.** concern **6.** childish

Jumpstart 12
Word of the Day: Check students' sentences for accurate usage of the term.
Sentence Mender: They took the bus to see their grandmother in Kansas.
Cursive Quote: Check students' handwriting for accuracy and legibility. Responses will vary.
Analogy of the Day: A; (example-class analogy) Check that students' answers are reasonable.
Ready, Set, Read! 1. She knew how much fun it was to get a card you didn't expect. **2.** Answers will vary; sample answer: They might feel lonely or tired, and they might miss their families.
Brainteaser:

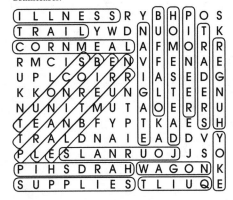

Morning Jumpstarts: Reading, Grade 4 © 2013 Scholastic Teaching Resources

Jumpstart 13

Word of the Day: Check students' sentences for accurate usage of the term.
Sentence Mender: Would you like butter or sour cream on your baked potato?
Cursive Quote: Check students' handwriting for accuracy and legibility. Responses will vary.
Analogy of the Day: D; (object-description analogy) Check that students' answers are reasonable.
Ready, Set, Read! 1. A **2.** D **3.** It probably got blown inside out.
Brainteaser: (Top to bottom) cloud, flute, hosts, kneel, pearl; fourth column: utter

Jumpstart 14

Word of the Day: Check students' sentences for accurate usage of the term.
Sentence Mender: We must start on time to finish the game by dark.
Cursive Quote: Check students' handwriting for accuracy and legibility. Responses will vary.
Analogy of the Day: B; (object-user analogy) Check that students' answers are reasonable.
Ready, Set, Read! 1. It is made only of snow. **2.** The spiral helps shape the dome; the angle of the blocks keeps the others in position. The weight of the blocks is also a factor.
Brainteaser: 1. not **2.** lets **3.** spoon **4.** bag **5.** money

Jumpstart 15

Word of the Day: Check students' sentences for accurate usage of the term.
Sentence Mender: Oh, my goodness! We won the raffle!
Cursive Quote: Check students' handwriting for accuracy and legibility. Responses will vary.
Analogy of the Day: A; (synonyms analogy) Check that students' answers are reasonable.
Ready, Set, Read! 1. Valo is a dragon who can't breathe fire. **2.** She tells him that when he gets older, he'll be able to. **3.** B
Brainteaser: 1. flute **2.** harp **3.** drums **4.** trumpet **5.** bagpipes **6.** trombone **7.** organ **8.** recorder **9.** guitar **10.** tambourine

Jumpstart 16

Word of the Day: Check students' sentences for accurate usage of the term.
Sentence Mender: Keep all knives away from small children.
Cursive Quote: Check students' handwriting for accuracy and legibility. Responses will vary.
Analogy of the Day: D; (part-whole analogy) Check that students' answers are reasonable.
Ready, Set, Read! 1. D **2.** Submarine crews give up a lot of comforts to do their jobs.
Brainteaser: Answers will vary; sample answers:

	B	E	S	T
Names of Cities	Boston	El Paso	Seattle	Tampa
Map Words	bridge	east	south	trail
Forest Things	bear	elm tree	squirrel	thorn
Kitchen Things	banana	eggbeater	skillet	toaster

Jumpstart 17

Word of the Day: Check students' sentences for accurate usage of the term.
Sentence Mender: "How do you say the word for homework in Spanish?" asked Betsy.
Cursive Quote: Check students' handwriting for accuracy and legibility. Responses will vary.
Analogy of the Day: D; (member-group analogy) Check that students' answers are reasonable.
Ready, Set, Read! 1. Answers will vary; sample answer: They all rhyme, they all have two lines; they all give a way to predict rain. **2.** Answers will vary; sample answer: The one about the drawers and door means it's humid, so rain is likely.
Brainteaser: 2. how/who **3.** saw/was **4.** won/now **5.** not/ton **6.** tub/but

Jumpstart 18

Word of the Day: Check students' sentences for accurate usage of the term.
Sentence Mender: Mom likes chocolate-covered cherries best of all candies.
Cursive Quote: Check students' handwriting for accuracy and legibility. Responses will vary.
Analogy of the Day: B; (object-function analogy) Check that students' answers are reasonable.
Ready, Set, Read! 1. Pigment is something in nature that contains color. **2.** D
Brainteaser: Answers will vary; check students' word lists.

Jumpstart 19

Word of the Day: Check students' sentences for accurate usage of the term.
Sentence Mender: Do you think there will be a fire drill today?
Cursive Quote: Check students' handwriting for accuracy and legibility. Responses will vary.
Analogy of the Day: C; (object-function analogy) Check that students' answers are reasonable.
Ready, Set, Read! 1. Answers will vary; sample answer: He might have eaten up all their cornmeal; he may have frightened or harmed the people. **2.** A
Brainteaser: 1. window **2.** knock **3.** gang **4.** edge **5.** trust **6.** loyal **7.** plump **8.** health **9.** rooster

Jumpstart 20

Word of the Day: Check students' sentences for accurate usage of the term.
Sentence Mender: He watched in horror as a green snake crept toward the tent.
Cursive Quote: Check students' handwriting for accuracy and legibility. Responses will vary.
Analogy of the Day: B; (object-description analogy) Check that students' answers are reasonable.
Ready, Set, Read! 1. An ant farm is a protected area where ants can be observed as they work and eat. **2.** Answers will vary; sample answer: They changed their minds when they noticed how interesting it was to watch the ants.
Brainteaser: 1. prey **2.** press **3.** pretty **4.** prefer **5.** pretend **6.** predict **7.** pretzel

Jumpstart 21

Word of the Day: Check students' sentences for accurate usage of the term.
Sentence Mender: "Be home by four o'clock," said Dad.
Cursive Quote: Check students' handwriting for accuracy and legibility. Responses will vary.
Analogy of the Day: A; (example-class analogy) Check that students' answers are reasonable.
Ready, Set, Read! 1. He suggests that Idaho potatoes are enormous. **2.** Answers will vary; sample answer: It makes the potato seem bigger than the state itself!
Brainteaser: 1. baste **2.** claws **3.** grown **4.** overdue

Jumpstart 22

Word of the Day: Check students' sentences for accurate usage of the term.
Sentence Mender: The book's silly title makes me laugh.
Cursive Quote: Check students' handwriting for accuracy and legibility. Responses will vary.
Analogy of the Day: C; (antonyms analogy) Check that students' answers are reasonable.
Ready, Set, Read! 1. D **2.** C
Brainteaser: (Top to bottom) pastel, frame, clay, felt, paint, crayon; tempera

Jumpstart 23

Word of the Day: Check students' sentences for accurate usage of the term.
Sentence Mender: "Strike three! You're out!" yelled the umpire.
Cursive Quote: Check students' handwriting for accuracy and legibility. Responses will vary.
Analogy of the Day: D; (synonyms analogy) Check that students' answers are reasonable.
Ready, Set, Read! 1. Answers will vary; sample answer: She needed to earn money for her family. **2.** She shares a small room in a boarding house near the mill.
Brainteaser: (Top to bottom) teach, those, titan, tower, truly; Henry

Jumpstart 24

Word of the Day: Check students' sentences for accurate usage of the term.
Sentence Mender: I know all the words to all five verses of "This Land Is Your Land."
Cursive Quote: Check students' handwriting for accuracy and legibility. Responses will vary.
Analogy of the Day: C; (example-class analogy) Check that students' answers are reasonable.
Ready, Set, Read! 1. It is used two different times (in two different amounts) in the recipe. **2.** It means to push and press it with your hands.
Brainteaser: 1. occupied **2.** following **3.** blossom **4.** calm **5.** false

Jumpstart 25

Word of the Day: Check students' sentences for accurate usage of the term.
Sentence Mender: Arthur Wynne made the first crossword puzzle in 1913.
Cursive Quote: Check students' handwriting for accuracy and legibility. Responses will vary.
Analogy of the Day: B; (object-function analogy) Check that students' answers are reasonable.
Ready, Set, Read! 1. 9 feet tall **2.** Answers will vary; sample answer: It had the exact same life span as the grandfather; they got it when he was born, and it stopped working when he died.
Brainteaser: The nine-letter word is hardcover; other words will vary, but must include R and have at least three letters.

Morning Jumpstarts: Reading, Grade 4 © 2013 Scholastic Teaching Resources

Jumpstart 26

Word of the Day: Check students' sentences for accurate usage of the term.
Sentence Mender: Ninth President William Henry Harrison served for less than thirty-one days.
Cursive Quote: Check students' handwriting for accuracy and legibility. Responses will vary.
Analogy of the Day: D; (antonyms analogy) Check that students' answers are reasonable.
Ready, Set, Read! 1. B **2.** He had only one hand.
Brainteaser: 1. lazy **2.** cozy **3.** zesty **4.** dozen **5.** breeze **6.** lizard

Jumpstart 27

Word of the Day: Check students' sentences for accurate usage of the term.
Sentence Mender: My uncle always sings a dumb song called "The Eggplant That Ate Chicago."
Cursive Quote: Check students' handwriting for accuracy and legibility. Responses will vary.
Analogy of the Day: B; (antonyms analogy) Check that students' answers are reasonable.
Ready, Set, Read! 1. D **2.** Answers will vary; sample answer: It teaches not to be greedy.
Brainteaser: 1. inning **2.** strike **3.** slugger **4.** bunt **5.** glove **6.** single **7.** steal **8.** triple **9.** mound **10.** fielder **11.** tag **12.** slide **13.** out **14.** catcher

Jumpstart 28

Word of the Day: Check students' sentences for accurate usage of the term.
Sentence Mender: Jamille passed the test and got the highest score of anybody.
Cursive Quote: Check students' handwriting for accuracy and legibility. Responses will vary.
Analogy of the Day: B; (part-whole analogy) Check that students' answers are reasonable.
Ready, Set, Read! 1. D **2.** A
Brainteaser: rummy, aye, moo; Are you my mom?

Jumpstart 29

Word of the Day: Check students' sentences for accurate usage of the term.
Sentence Mender: "Where were you on Saturday, June 16, 2012, Dr. Miller?"
Cursive Quote: Check students' handwriting for accuracy and legibility. Responses will vary.
Analogy of the Day: A; (object-description analogy) Check that students' answers are reasonable.
Ready, Set, Read! 1. Molly **2.** The dog really can talk!
Brainteaser: 2. ring **3.** web **4.** basket **5.** oil **6.** pen

Jumpstart 30

Word of the Day: Check students' sentences for accurate usage of the term.
Sentence Mender: Can you believe that Alaska has a town called Y?
Cursive Quote: Check students' handwriting for accuracy and legibility. Responses will vary.
Analogy of the Day: D; (user-object analogy) Check that students' answers are reasonable.
Ready, Set, Read! 1. B **2.** A longer didj makes a lower tone; a shorter didj makes a higher tone.
Brainteaser: Answers may vary; sample answers: **1.** drain **2.** latch **3.** birdseed **4.** eraser **5.** timer **6.** soapdish **7.** folder **8.** mailbox **9.** playground **10.** pinecone

Jumpstart 31

Word of the Day: Check students' sentences for accurate usage of the term.
Sentence Mender: They shouldn't play their music so loud when kids are trying to sleep.
Cursive Quote: Check students' handwriting for accuracy and legibility. Responses will vary.
Analogy of the Day: A; (cause-and-effect analogy) Check that students' answers are reasonable.
Ready, Set, Read! 1. B **2.** Answers will vary; sample answer: It was during the day, so the room wasn't dark!
Brainteaser: Answers will vary; check students' nouns.

Jumpstart 32

Word of the Day: Check students' sentences for accurate usage of the term.
Sentence Mender: Stephen Foster, the great American songwriter, was born on July 4, 1828.
Cursive Quote: Check students' handwriting for accuracy and legibility. Responses will vary.
Analogy of the Day: B; (object-function analogy) Check that students' answers are reasonable.
Ready, Set, Read! 1. The words in italics are Dr. Earle's own words. **2.** Answers will vary; sample answer: Without all that the ocean provides us, nothing on Earth would grow.
Brainteaser: Answers will vary; check students' verbs.

Jumpstart 33

Word of the Day: Check students' sentences for accurate usage of the term.
Sentence Mender: "May I please have your autograph, Prince William?"
Cursive Quote: Check students' handwriting for accuracy and legibility. Responses will vary.
Analogy of the Day: A; (antonyms analogy) Check that students' answers are reasonable.
Ready, Set, Read! 1. B **2.** Verse 1: all things that show their beauty in speed; verse 2: all things that show their beauty in slowness. 3. It means powerful.
Brainteaser: Answers will vary; sample answer: Horrible Helen has hungry hamsters helping her hoist her helicopter.

Jumpstart 34

Word of the Day: Check students' sentences for accurate usage of the term.
Sentence Mender: Our summer garden in full bloom is as pretty as a picture.
Cursive Quote: Check students' handwriting for accuracy and legibility. Responses will vary.
Analogy of the Day: C; (degree of meaning or synonyms analogy) Check that students' answers are reasonable.
Ready, Set, Read! 1. B **2.** A
Brainteaser: Answers may vary; sample answer: cork, conk, honk, hunk

Jumpstart 35

Word of the Day: Check students' sentences for accurate usage of the term.
Sentence Mender: Let's put some beans, cucumbers, cheese, and beets in the salad. Note: the series comma before *and* is optional.
Cursive Quote: Check students' handwriting for accuracy and legibility. Responses will vary.
Analogy of the Day: B; (part-whole analogy) Check that students' answers are reasonable.
Ready, Set, Read! 1. Answers will vary; sample answers: 1) Tornadoes are violent storms that twist; 2) the Grand Canyon was once filled with water; 3) Death Valley is below sea level and is in California. **2.** D
Brainteaser: (Top to bottom) 3, 7, 6, 2, 1, 4, 5

Jumpstart 36

Word of the Day: Check students' sentences for accurate usage of the term.
Sentence Mender: Whose winter coat has lost its hood?
Cursive Quote: Check students' handwriting for accuracy and legibility. Responses will vary.
Analogy of the Day: C; (part-whole analogy) Check that students' answers are reasonable.
Ready, Set, Read! 1. Answers will vary; sample answer: It can help them be less embarrassed about having no hair. **2.** The writer includes Anthony's very own words.
Brainteaser: finds, sash, hip; fish and ships

Jumpstart 37

Word of the Day: Check students' sentences for accurate usage of the term.
Sentence Mender: Which one of these new songs did you like the least?
Cursive Quote: Check students' handwriting for accuracy and legibility. Responses will vary.
Analogy of the Day: D; (doer-action analogy) Check that students' answers are reasonable.
Ready, Set, Read! 1. C **2.** Answers will vary; sample answer: Perhaps that would be a better, safer, easier, more respected job.
Brainteaser: Answers will vary; check students' word lists.

Jumpstart 38

Word of the Day: Check students' sentences for accurate usage of the term.
Sentence Mender: It's totally impossible to keep your eyes open when you sneeze.
Cursive Quote: Check students' handwriting for accuracy and legibility. Responses will vary.
Analogy of the Day: C; (object-description analogy) Check that students' answers are reasonable.
Ready, Set, Read! 1. This was a way to show mutual trust. **2.** The author tells where it came from in history, and gives a modern example.
Brainteaser: (Top to bottom) at, ate, team, meant, mental, mantels, ailments

Jumpstart 39
Word of the Day: Check students' sentences for accurate usage of the term.
Sentence Mender: An ostrich's eye is bigger than its brain!
Cursive Quote: Check students' handwriting for accuracy and legibility. Responses will vary.
Analogy of the Day: D; (antonyms analogy) Check that students' answers are reasonable.
Ready, Set, Read! 1. Jaguar had weapons and fire, which the humans did not.
2. Answers will vary; sample answer: Jaguar showed kindness to the man, but the man repaid his kindness with cruelty. That made them enemies.
Brainteaser:

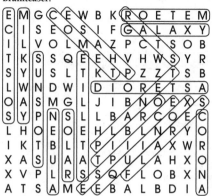

Jumpstart 40
Word of the Day: Check students' sentences for accurate usage of the term.
Sentence Mender: The world's heaviest onion weighed more than a man's head!
Cursive Quote: Check students' handwriting for accuracy and legibility. Responses will vary.
Analogy of the Day: A; (example-class analogy) Check that students' answers are reasonable.
Ready, Set, Read! 1. A prequel is a story that comes before the original story.
2. They can keep readers interested by making the story unpredictable, and giving it lots of variety.
Brainteaser: 1. ten/net **2.** gel/leg **3.** den/end **4.** war/raw **5.** Sue/use **6.** Now/own

Jumpstart 41
Word of the Day: Check students' sentences for accurate usage of the term.
Sentence Mender: Each tiger has unique stripes, almost like people have fingerprints.
Cursive Quote: Check students' handwriting for accuracy and legibility. Responses will vary.
Analogy of the Day: B; (object-user analogy) Check that students' answers are reasonable.
Ready, Set, Read! 1. C **2.** Both are designs worn on the skin; but mehndi are temporary and are painted on.
Brainteaser: 1. ajar **2.** jazz **3.** eject **4.** major **5.** banjo **6.** enjoy **7.** object

Jumpstart 42
Word of the Day: Check students' sentences for accurate usage of the term.
Sentence Mender: Yesterday she was too sick to go to school, but today she is better.
Cursive Quote: Check students' handwriting for accuracy and legibility. Responses will vary.
Analogy of the Day: C; (part-whole analogy) Check that students' answers are reasonable.
Ready, Set, Read! 1. D **2.** The list explains the different customs for each of the five days of Diwali.
Brainteaser: Answers will vary; check students' adjectives.

Jumpstart 43
Word of the Day: Check students' sentences for accurate usage of the term.
Sentence Mender: Yes, Jared practices his piano lesson for fifteen minutes a day.
Cursive Quote: Check students' handwriting for accuracy and legibility. Responses will vary.
Analogy of the Day: B; (object-description analogy) Check that students' answers are reasonable.
Ready, Set, Read! 1. D **2.** C
Brainteaser: (Top to bottom) 5, 7, 2, 3, 4, 1, 6

Jumpstart 44
Word of the Day: Check students' sentences for accurate usage of the term.
Sentence Mender: Her truly favorite athlete is soccer player David Beckham.
Cursive Quote: Check students' handwriting for accuracy and legibility. Responses will vary.
Analogy of the Day: D; (synonyms analogy) Check that students' answers are reasonable.
Ready, Set, Read! 1. The triangles equally represent the three parts of complete health.
2. C
Brainteaser: 1. or **2.** word **3.** tower **4.** belt **5.** a **6.** and

Jumpstart 45
Word of the Day: Check students' sentences for accurate usage of the term.
Sentence Mender: Please leave your suitcase here while you buy your ticket.
Cursive Quote: Check students' handwriting for accuracy and legibility. Responses will vary.
Analogy of the Day: D; (example-class analogy) Check that students' answers are reasonable.
Ready, Set, Read! 1. Henry thought the assignment would be quick and easy.
2. His attitude changed once he began to look closely and carefully at the space inside the frame.
Brainteaser: 1. cape **2.** recap **3.** caper **4.** escape **5.** hubcap **6.** caption **7.** capital **8.** captain

Jumpstart 46
Word of the Day: Check students' sentences for accurate usage of the term.
Sentence Mender: We finished two whole watermelons at the class picnic.
Cursive Quote: Check students' handwriting for accuracy and legibility. Responses will vary.
Analogy of the Day: A; (part-whole analogy) Check that students' answers are reasonable.
Ready, Set, Read! 1. B **2.** D
Brainteaser: 1. blood **2.** wood **3.** tongue **4.** thumb **5.** shine **6.** piece **7.** now **8.** kick **9.** start **10.** hold

Jumpstart 47
Word of the Day: Check students' sentences for accurate usage of the term.
Sentence Mender: Lake Huron is the fourth deepest of the five Great Lakes.
Cursive Quote: Check students' handwriting for accuracy and legibility. Responses will vary.
Analogy of the Day: C; (part-whole analogy) Check that students' answers are reasonable.
Ready, Set, Read! 1. They didn't always understand how the world worked, so they blamed things on spirits and fairies instead. **2.** C
Brainteaser: Answers will vary; sample answer: Yellowstone, Endicott, Texas, Springfield, Delaware, Easton, Nevada . . .

Jumpstart 48
Word of the Day: Check students' sentences for accurate usage of the term.
Sentence Mender: The axolotl, or Mexican walking fish, we know as a salamander.
Cursive Quote: Check students' handwriting for accuracy and legibility. Responses will vary.
Analogy of the Day: C; (degree of meaning or synonyms analogy) Check that students' answers are reasonable.
Ready, Set, Read! 1. Supreme Court **2.** Legislative **3.** B
Brainteaser: read, shack, scrape; chase parked cars

Jumpstart 49
Word of the Day: Check students' sentences for accurate usage of the term.
Sentence Mender: He likes his iced tea with a lot of sugar or honey.
Cursive Quote: Check students' handwriting for accuracy and legibility. Responses will vary.
Analogy of the Day: B; (object-location analogy) Check that students' answers are reasonable.
Ready, Set, Read! 1. The narrator was trying to make noise so any nearby wild animals wouldn't be surprised. **2.** Answers will vary; sample answer: It means to stay near to the water's edge. **3.** D
Brainteaser: 1. waist **2.** wring **3.** oar **4.** hoarse **5.** lead **6.** manes **7.** patients

Jumpstart 50
Word of the Day: Check students' sentences for accurate usage of the term.
Sentence Mender: Sorry, son, but you aren't the one who gets to decide.
Cursive Quote: Check students' handwriting for accuracy and legibility. Responses will vary.
Analogy of the Day: A; (cause-and-effect analogy) Check that students' answers are reasonable.
Ready, Set, Read! 1. Great Britain **2.** It is named for the cooking sounds of the potatoes.
Brainteaser: Answers will vary; sample answers:

	F	E	L	T
Foods	French fries	eggs	lettuce	tuna
Nations	Fiji	Egypt	Laos	Tanzania
Movies	Finding Nemo	E.T.	Lady and the Tramp	Toy Story
Mammals	fox	elephant	lynx	tiger

Morning Jumpstarts: Reading, Grade 4 © 2013 Scholastic Teaching Resources